Happening in Education — Theoretical Issues

GDAŃSK STUDIES IN LANGUAGE

Edited by Danuta Stanulewicz

VOLUME 13

PETER LANG
EDITION

Martin Blaszk

Happening in Education — Theoretical Issues

PETER LANG
EDITION

Bibliographic Information published by the Deutsche Nationalbibliothek
The Deutsche Nationalbibliothek lists this publication in the Deutsche Nationalbibliografie; detailed bibliographic data is available in the internet at http://dnb.d-nb.de.
Library of Congress Cataloging-in-Publication Data
Names: Blaszk, Martin, author.
Title: Happening in education : theoretical issues / Martin Blaszk.
2
Description: Frankfurt am Main ; New York : Peter Lang, [2017] | Series: Gda?nsk studies in language, ISSN 2196-016X ; vol. 13 | Includes bibliographical references and index.
Identifiers: LCCN 2017020638| ISBN 9783631722428 (print) | ISBN 9783631722435
((E-PDF) | ISBN 9783631722442 (EPUB) | ISBN 9783631722459 (MOBI)
Subjects: LCSH: Teaching--Experimental methods. | Critical pedagogy.
Classification: LCC LB1027.3 .B55 2017 | DDC 370.11/5--dc23 LC record available at https://lccn.loc.gov/2017020638

This publication was financially supported by the University of Gdańsk.

ISSN 2196-016X
ISBN 978-3-631-72242-8 (Print)
E-ISBN 978-3-631-72243-5 (E-Book)
E-ISBN 978-3-631-72244-2 (EPUB)
E-ISBN 978-3-631-72245-9 (MOBI)
DOI 10.3726/b11112

Peter Lang Edition is an Imprint of Peter Lang GmbH.

Peter Lang – Frankfurt am Main · Bern · Bruxelles · New York · Oxford · Warszawa · Wien

This publication has been peer reviewed.

www.peterlang.com

Acknowledgements

I would like to thank everyone who has made it possible for me to carry out my research and write this book. These include people I work with in teaching and creating happenings, as well as students and academic staff at the University of Gdańsk. Special thanks go to the following individuals: Dorota Klus-Stańska, Maria Mendel, Katarzyna Krasoń, Danuta Stanulewicz, Michael John James Brown, Anna Wróbel, Magdalena Wawrzyniak-Śliwska, Zbigniew Czaja and Grażyna Zawisza.

I also want to thank Beata and Ewa for the patience, support and good humour they have shown throughout my work on this project.

Contents

List of illustrations

All illustrations by the author.

Introduction

Why happening and why education? A simple answer to these questions is that I have been involved in both areas for over twenty years as a practitioner, and so it is perhaps inevitable that they should form the centre of interest for a research project. Indeed, my initial training is as a visual artist (although not in performance studies), while my involvement in teaching and education came a little later, primarily as a means to an end; I wanted to travel, especially to Poland, so taking up English teaching as a "second" profession seemed the ideal way for me to move around, earn a living and also continue to pursue and develop an art practice.

These are not the only reasons, however. Being involved in both areas almost simultaneously, I could notice how one fed into the other, as a result of which, over the years, I became increasingly interested in how they affected one another. In addition to this, I was fortunate enough to start my teaching career proper, and this, I must repeat, is a career in teaching English abroad, and mostly, as has turned out in Poland, in an institution and at a time when experimentation and risk-taking were very much encouraged and supported. Therefore, working at the then English Language Centre at the University of Gdańsk, which was supported and part-funded by the British Council, allowed me to start my teaching career with a group of professionals and in a place where the performative aspects of teaching English were as encouraged in their formation and exploration as were the formal aspects of teaching English as a foreign language. This meant that teaching the English language was as much about how it was taught as the language itself. Neither should this come as any great surprise, because the British tradition of teaching English as a foreign language was and is based on a humanistic tradition that takes into account the social and psychological as much the linguistic. It is also eclectic in nature, not adhering to one overriding method or approach but rather trying to find connections between those that are available, first and foremost to satisfy the needs of the learners rather than to pursue a particular pedagogical agenda. This has meant that throughout my career as a teacher, and then later a teacher trainer, I have constantly been engaged with people involved in learning: negotiating and facilitating that process. It has also meant an awareness that the factors which make up and inform the teaching process go beyond simply imparting knowledge about a particular subject area.

0.1. Happening and education

That happening can be linked to education in the first place should come as no surprise. Neither should my attempts to find a place for it within education. One of its main proponents, Allan Kaprow, promoted such a link. For him, it was one of the ways in which he might lead "a philosophical inquiry into the given natural/or social 'forms' of common experience" (Kelly 2003: xvii), while the publication of a number of articles on this point, *The Education of the Un-Artist, Parts I, II,* and *III* (Kelly 2003: 97–126; 130–147), were meant to provide guidance. In addition to this, many of the performance practices that have been described as leading up to and away from happening in terms of a chronological history (Goldberg 1990), have had educational connections, or at least aspirations. Therefore, Dada, the Italian and Russian Futurists and Bauhaus, as well as contemporary performance art, might be said to have had, and have, in one way or another, an educational purpose: be it in the fields of the aesthetic, the social and/or the political.

Additionally, trying to locate this type of expression, which might be termed ludic and contestational, within education is nothing new. My own attempt to find a place for it is perhaps not that far removed from the deliberations of the town officials in Britain 500 years ago, when they wanted to find a way to utilize performance practices of the time, clerical, but also ludic, for purposes that would be beneficial to the population as a whole. As Clopper (2001: 159) writes, "they were expected to entertain citizens [...] and they were expected to provide a moral example", but overall, "the plays [performative practices – MB] were intended to educate and confirm laymen in their religion".

But what exactly are the educational discourses that happening might be said to be linked to? And what are the links? The answer, it seems to me, stems in part from its history, which is apparent even from the very brief description I have given above: the aesthetic, social, and political, open up a broad area of inquiry that connect with the fundamental concerns of happening, translate into its characteristics, and can be seen to connect with various discourses in education at the present time. A summary glance over some of the characteristics and strategies open to happening as a performative practice would appear to uphold this. For example, the characteristic that calls for an abolishment of borders between the arts, the interdisciplinary nature of happening, places it on an aesthetic plane. Additionally, so does the possibility for nonmatrixed presentations and compartmentalization, so that people do not have to take on roles, or actually present actions or events that are related in any way, being involved in sequences that encompass dream-like rather than conscious thinking (Schechner 1982: 122–123).

In this challenge to existing order and the possibilities for a series of narratives rather than one leading narrative, there is also a critical element, as well as a relation to postmodern discourse. In addition to this, these aesthetic-critical concerns cum characteristics, might also be seen to correspond to a spectrum of educational discourses. The nonmatrixed and interdisciplinary character of happening can be equated to the independence and freedom from limitations that Szmidt (2007: 51) refers to with regard to a pedagogy of creativity, or the autonomy and freedom that Sajdak (2008: 55) proposes for creative education. It can also be related to the continuous and reciprocal process Nęcka (1994: 21) writes about for creativity, where there is not one particular, nor imposed form or procedure, and where structure is revealed by the movement through an interaction of the person with materials and events in the steady evolvement of an idea and the aim to be achieved. And these forms of involvement also have a political undercurrent regarding the challenge they offer to both accepted order and control.

In addition to this, the social strand of happening is represented by the emphasis that is placed upon participation, where, at its weakest, the audience are responsible for creating meaning (Goldberg 1990: 130), or at its strongest, the audience takes part along with the happeners in the enactment of the happening (Pawłowski 1982: 74–77). This, in turn, allows for further strategies for performance that Schechner (1982: 120–121) outlines: relational involvement, in that no-one – neither happeners nor audience – have a privileged position with regard to ideas and decisions; and multicentrism, where those taking part can present different viewpoints. And again, as with the aesthetic dimension, there are currents inherent in these strategies that connect with the political regarding their critical-emancipatory possibilities. This social element also shows itself in another proposed characteristic for happening: that it should be anything but the arts (Kaprow 1994: 706), that it should, in fact, be of real life (Vostell cited in Heddon and Milling 2006: 66); that is, any one of the myriad of activities and involvements that people engage in on a day to day basis (Kaprow 2003: 64–65). In terms of educational discourses, the creation of a situation where people can come together and express different ideas occurs in Garoian's (1999: 40–43) proposition of a liminal space for performance art pedagogy, as well as in Witkowski's (2000: 15) consideration of border pedagogy, where there is an intensive relation with the other person. Moreover, the disparate forms this relation can take and the fact that different points of view are represented recall Rutkowiak's (1997: 88–98) ideas concerning "the outsider", in which four possibilities are outlined: we can try to get to know the other person, see ourselves more clearly in comparison to them, try not to lose sight of who that other person actually is, and/or, where the other person is important in our self-education. This and the positioning of happening in real life rather than the arts connect with Dewey's call to find inspiration in the everyday. And this is not only in his writing about the arts (Dewey 1958), which was a major inspiration for Kaprow,[1] but also his project for education (Dewey 1956, 1966), in which school and society are inextricably entwined. This is a project, moreover, that has been continued into the present through the likes of Bruner (1999) and his work around cultural psychology, and in Poland, through the research of Klus-Stańska (2002).

The mention of Dewey here also offers a link between the social and the political. For the likes of Melosik (2007: 311–316), Dewey's pragmatism is an attempt to resolve the problem between individual development and social integration that lies at the heart of compulsory education in liberal-capitalist societies. For Szudlarek (2009: 65) and the critical pedagogy that he writes about, Dewey offers a vision that joins the pedagogical and the political, providing a mechanism which enables the formation of a truly democratic society. This, in turn, is echoed in Matynia's (2009) proposal for performative democracy, where at a grassroots level, people come together and reach consensus on matters that are significant for them, and on from that, are able to put those ideas into action and for (significant) change.

Of course, what I am presenting here are only a very few of the possibilities that are apparent from the most cursory of glances. In the main body of the text I will expand upon these ideas further.

0.2. Performance art and devising

With such a history, a problem I have had from the very beginning of this project is the choice of terminology open to me, especially in relation to the main focus of my inquiry – happening. Indeed, is the word *happening* (and the set of

---

1 In the introduction to an anthology of Kaprow's writings from throughout his career, Jeff Kelley places Dewey as central to Kaprow's thinking and art, starting as a young artist right up to the latter years of his practice. One short passage at the beginning of his text shows the inevitability almost, of such a situation. Kelley (2003: xi) writes of Kaprow's earliest contact with Dewey's *Art as Experience*: "in it, around 1949, the young, ambitious artist and philosophy graduate student pencilled in his thoughts as he read, [...] these inscriptions [...] carry a certain weight, like subheadings for pages not yet written. One feels in them the tug of re-cognition as it pulls the artist away from the philosopher's text and toward the margins, where his own thinking begins to take shape. With these and other scribbles, Kaprow grounds himself in American pragmatism and forecasts the themes of his career".

concepts it implies) the most appropriate to apply to (a) the arts practice I am involved in and trying to describe, and (b) what I am advocating as a practice suitable for education? With reference to arts practice, this has been (and, I suspect, will continue to be) an extremely pertinent question, as I have, at times, labelled myself as performance artist or live artist,[2] as well as seeing myself as involved in happenings. What the differences might be and whether or not they have a significant impact on the work carried out is open to question. Indeed, my unwillingness to try and be too "determinist" on this point can be seen in my discussion of happening in Chapter 2, where I describe its genesis in a visual arts tradition, its possibilities as theatre and non-theatre, as well as its ties to either the modern or post-modern. It is also apparent in an empirical study (Blaszk 2017), where participants were encouraged to research the phenomenon for themselves, share the ideas they found, and then build towards a happening through group discussion and action.

Meanwhile, in my discussion of happening in this book, I bring in ideas related to performance art, and in the area of education, performance art pedagogy which, I feel, help to explain and define more clearly the particular type of happening I am involved in and trying to establish for education, but, at the same time, may not "fit in" with other, more mainstream views. Of course, this does raise the question of whether I am simply involved in performance art and/or devising by another name, something older and by now surely obsolete? This might seem to be the case when taking into account the moves in America to establish performance more firmly as an academic discipline (Spencer 2001: 100), or when one reads about happening in two authoritative histories, where it is seen as either a bit player in an overall and seemingly inevitable development towards performance art (Goldberg 1990) or as part and parcel of the history of devising (Heddon and Milling 2006). I would argue that these are not the only ways of viewing happening, however, and that by trying to tie it down in the ways these particular narratives do is to deny its possibilities as a still relevant and vital force.

Mention of these issues also brings up further reasons for choosing to use the term *happening* and not some other. And this is to do with the Polish context within which I am carrying out my research and writing, as well as the fact that happening, or rather the term *happening*, has always been an unstable entity. In

2 This, however, has been as much a matter of geographical location and tradition as personal choice. In Poland in the mid 1990s, for instance, performance artist was used, while in Britain it was the term *live artist*. I accepted whichever label was being used.

relation to the Polish context, the power of happening is witnessed in its present-day use by performers and non-performers alike: the happenings of the Polish group *Teatr Strefa Ciszy*, and in society in general, actions carried out by various Polish politicians, particularly Janusz Palikot and Jarosław Kaczyński. In other countries, Britain and America, for example, I would argue this is not the case. However, other phenomena, such as flashmob and the various street sit-ins or protests that are enabled by communications technology and the ubiquitous social media, might be said to be related to the happening tradition, as well as a continuation of it, encouraging as they do participation, their one-off nature and their seeming show of spontaneity.[3]

Additionally, when it comes to contemporary arts practices in Britain and America, the terms *live art*, *performance art*, or *devising* are preferred. To detail all of the reasons for this is beyond the scope of this particular study, although it might be guessed that the dynamic of change in these particular countries, as well as the fact that the term *happening* itself was never felt to be a very satisfactory label for this type of practice, have influenced the situation. On both counts, Kaprow, one of the very first happeners, and the person to first use the term *happening* in relation to performance practice, makes comments that suggest this to be the case. In the opening lines from an article written in 1979, he writes: "Coming into happening in the late fifties, I was certain the goal was to 'do' an art that was distinct from any known genre (or combination of genres). It seemed important to develop something that was not another type of painting, literature, music, dance, theater, opera" (Kelly 2003: 195). Meanwhile, thirteen years earlier, in a description of his own work for Michael Kirby (1966: 47), he admitted: "The name 'happening' is unfortunate. It was not intended to stand for an art form, originally. It was merely a neutral word that was part of a title of one of my projected ideas in 1958–59. It was the word which I thought would get me

3 For an informative and early account of the flash mob phenomenon see Wasik (2006: 56–66). The originator of flash mob, Bill Wasik does not mention any link to happening or performance at all. He describes it as social-scientific enquiry, citing the social psychologist Stanley Milgram and his experiments on authority as an inspiration. He also states that flash mob was supposed to be a temporary phenomenon, with no real purpose other than to be "a metaphor for the hollow hipster culture that spawned it" (Wasik 2006: 57). Apart from flash mob being described as funny, aesthetic and social, a political edge is also suggested with links to Howard Rheingold's *Smart Mobs: The Next Social revolution* (Wasik 2006: 64). Indeed, this idea is given more credence by another author writing at the very start of the phenomenon – see Shmueli (2003).

out of trouble of calling it a 'theatre piece,' a 'performance,' a 'game,' a 'total art,' or whatever, that would not evoke associations with known sports, theatre and so on". Finally, the term *happening* and the concepts that relate to it are also closer to what I am actually involved in as an arts practitioner, and as one of the purposes of the research is to inquire into happening in education whilst, at the same time, develop it as a practice, it seems appropriate to work within an area that I know and continue to work within.

0.3. Outline of chapters

The book as a whole is divided into six chapters. In Chapter 1, a background to the inquiry is provided. In doing so, a number of perspectives on contemporary society are presented followed by a consideration of how schooling (compulsory education) is seen to fit into this wider picture. Additionally, an outline of some of the demands placed upon education by present-day society is given, as well as some of the difficulties that exist which make fulfilling these demands problematic. To end the chapter, happening as a possibility in education is offered.

With Chapter 2, an account of happening is provided in which its complex and contradictory nature is shown: where it is viewed as an art form based within the visual arts, a form of theatre, or anything but arts orientated, taking its inspiration from "real life". In addition to this, a provenance for happening in modernism is established as well as its possibilities as part of a postmodern project, still being used by artists (and not only artists) up into the present time. Moreover, to gain a fuller understanding of its functioning, a number of salient characteristics for happening are defined, such as participation, its nonmatrixed character and the abolition of borders between art forms. In connection with this, happening is proposed as a form with aesthetic-critical possibilities, as well as being "sensitive" to location.

The first steps to place happening within an educational setting occur in Chapter 3. To do this, traits of liminal space are used as a means of encompassing and developing considerations concerning the possibilities for happening and education in connection with a number of areas. These include the sociopolitical sphere, concerning performative democracy and border pedagogy as well as critical pedagogy and the emancipatory project it promotes. Happening is also analysed with regard to the individual and others in connection with educational practice. Additionally, a consideration of the objectification that occurs in happening is undertaken. Completing the chapter, liminality is viewed in relation to two educational studies and what these tell us about the space of happening.

In Chapter 4, happening's ambivalent relationship with the theatre and its basis in the arts form the starting point for a comparison to drama pedagogy. This analysis is continued in relation to two constructivist models of learning as well as creative pedagogy. In addition, a psychological model for creativity is used to suggest how happening might function in an educational setting. Following on from this, creativity and how it is actually received within Polish schools at present is explored, as a point from which to view the (possible) reception of happening. Additionally, a happening-type practice from early education in Poland and one from the secondary sector in America are reviewed in terms of their application in those sectors respectively. A number of issues that arise from their use are also examined.

Moving on to Chapter 5, a research strategy for happening in education is outlined. In doing so, the aims of the research are given followed by an examination of two strategies that were first of all considered and then rejected: ethnodrama and action research. This is followed by a presentation of bricolage as a research strategy and why it is best suited as a method to inquire into happening in education. In addition to this, an innovative approach to the use of bricolage is described, based upon a version of Guattari and Deleuze's rhizome – a rhizome-tumbleweed. Descriptions of the strategy, research methods and techniques used are also given, followed by a brief consideration of the form, place and duration for a research project which was implemented.

In the Conclusion, a number of ideas presented in the previous chapters are drawn together to develop a discussion concerning the possibilities for happening within an educational setting.

1. The contemporary world, education, schooling and happening

In this chapter, the aim is to provide a background to the inquiry. A number of perspectives on the contemporary world are presented, followed by a consideration of how schooling (compulsory education) is seen to fit into this broader picture. This reconstruction of the cultural context is important because I believe happening, as well as being part of the contemporary world, also has a great deal to offer it, especially in relation to education where it could facilitate learner (participant) involvement in learning "akin" to the world, which more traditional forms of education do not. In line with this, therefore, after presenting some of the demands placed upon schooling by contemporary society, including some of the problems that exist in connection with these demands, some alternatives to traditional education are given. These, in turn, are believed to fulfil the requirements placed on education more successfully than traditional models of schooling. Finally, happening is offered as a possibility to be considered in relation to education.

1.1. The contemporary world

The contemporary world is an **ever-changing**, **unstable** place, one of **multiple voices** and **uncertainty**, where life has gone from being like a pilgrimage in which, according to Zygmunt Bauman (1993: 10, translation – MB), "the place of arrival is set beforehand", to a life of wandering "without any prior set direction" (Bauman 1993: 16, translation – MB). The flow of time has also been disrupted, so that instead of being a continuous process it has become a number of episodes, which can be taken as following on from one another, but more than likely run concurrently, or have no relation to one another whatsoever (Bauman 1993: 13). In such a situation, Bauman (1993: 18–29) tries to find a metaphor, a personification for the postmodern condition but has problems settling for one adequate to the task. Instead, he reaches for types from throughout history whom he recasts in a new light: the *flaneur*, the vagrant, the tourist and the player, types previously seen as marginal, now take centre stage as representatives of the postmodern era.[4]

4 The *flaneur* offers freedom from the demands imposed by others and of the imagination, a person for whom the world is a spectacle that can be watched but not necessarily engaged with; the vagrant has freedom of choice concerning the road (both literally

More recently, Bauman (2011: 40–41, translation – MB) has opted for a more encompassing embodiment of the times, one which is as swift moving and flexible in its ability to change as the times themselves: "Time indeed passes and the real art here depends on being able to keep pace with it. If you do not want to drown, surf persistently, that is, change as often as you are able, your wardrobe, furniture, wallpaper, your look and habits, in short – yourself".

This ability to be someone else, to pose, is also something Ulrich Beck comments upon in his exploration of contemporary society as one where **risk plays a central role**. However, whereas Bauman's posing involves constantly changing oneself to feel in control, the posing Beck (2003: 10–15) describes is the necessity to show oneself to be in control of what is, in effect, uncontrollable in connection with both the dangers of the natural and the industrial world. This is a result of the success of industrial society, which having done away with any form of opposition (antithesis) is now left on its own to deal with itself. This reflexive position with regard to its own development, leading, as Beck would have it, to a "loss of innocence", where the risks of production both to the environment and humanity, which were once something hidden, have become an acknowledged part of continuing modernization. On the one hand, this means that risk is placed at the centre of modern / postmodern experience, along with the pose of control, while on the other, it has a created a situation in which "modernization has *consumed and lost its other* and now undermines its own premises as an industrial society along with its functional principles" (Beck 2003: 10). This has resulted in a situation where important elements which are/were part of industrial society have all now been undermined or even destroyed, one where

> People are *set free* from the certainties and modes of living of the industrial epoch [...] The system of coordinates in which life and thinking are fastened in industrial modernity – the axes of gender, family and occupation, the belief in science and progress – begins to shake, and a new twilight of opportunities and hazards comes into existence – the contours of the risk society. (Beck 2003: 14–15)

Moving on from Beck, the responsibility to control that which cannot really be controlled, is viewed on the personal, existential level by Lech Witkowski. He

---

and metaphorically) that she/he takes; the tourist is like the nineteenth century anthropologist who thirsts for adventure and new experiences to add to her/his collection, "to enrich the strong room of his impressions" (Bauman 1993: 25, translation – MB). Finally, the player is someone for whom the whole of life is a game, in which sometimes one wins and sometimes one loses, and where nothing is written for definite except the continuation of the game itself.

sees the contemporary world as no longer offering a "universe of culture outside of the person" but rather a world "of the interior, of the person by themselves, who with growing difficulty builds his own existential values" (Witkowski 2007: 61, translation – MB). In analysing the postmodern condition further, Witkowski cites the work of the poet Tadeusz Różewicz. However, in contrast to Różewicz's vision of a person who is falling, which is a symbol of the modern era from the first half of the twentieth century, Witkowski (2007: 56, translation – MB) proposes an image in which **the person is falling to pieces**:

> From [...] [which] is born the problem of building the integral self, one's own self, the feeling that you know yourself, who you are, and that you are in possession of the feeling that you have a worthy identity. It is at the same time the problem of the possibility of building your own integral biography from remains, biographical fragments, roles from fragmented repertoires, chance contacts, fragmented experience.

Witkowski (2007: 57, translation – MB) follows this with a description of the actions of this person, "the defenceless SELF", which "are often auto-destructive and aggressive. [They also involve t]he dramatic building of an interactive space, searching for the possibility of finding oneself in the world".

A continuation of this more radical point of view is presented by Tomasz Szkudlarek (Szkudlarek and Śliwerski 1991: 64–65, translation – MB), who sees "the world of human consciousness [...] [as] a world of constant conflicts, a constant rubbing up against various, fragmented and incomplete discourses presenting fragmented human involvement in fragmented contexts of reality". This is a world filtered through the vision of Michel Foucault, within which

> Instead of "facts" [...] we have rather contact with an "archaeological dig", whose every shard and fragment is involved in a different narrative, a different social context, a different discourse. Narratives can be constructed around each of them – but they will never form one History. (Szkudlarek and Śliwerski 1991: 65–66, translation – MB)

Indeed, in accordance with Foucault's ideas relating to subjectivity, each individual is responsible for building their own identity through the continuous negotiation and re-negotiation of power / knowledge structures that make up their world at any given time. This element of negotiation is vital if the subject is not to become engulfed by norms that do not allow growth and development, either in the individual themselves but also in their relations to others. There is, therefore, a critical dimension where the individual needs to be aware of the possibilities inherent in the different choices she/he makes so as to benefit from them as fully as possible. Indeed, Dianne Taylor (2011: 173) writes that for Foucault

> subjectivity is not distinct from but is rather formed in and through relations of power. There are not emancipatory institutions and norms that enable us, on the one hand, and

> oppressive or normalizing institutions and norms that constrain us, on the other; rather, we are simultaneously enabled and constrained by the same institutions and norms. We therefore find ourselves confronted with the task of figuring out when and how we are enabled and when and how we are constrained, of determining ways in which existing practices have the potential to loosen constraints and thus resist normalization, and of employing those practices not only for that purpose, but also in order to develop new and different practices – new and different ways of relating to ourselves and others. We need, in other words, to be able to reflect critically on the very process of becoming a subject.

It is also important to note that this finding of oneself does not lead to the uncovering of a "one true self", but **a process of uncovering** which involves *insubordination*. Therefore, "it is a matter of calling into question such an understanding of what it means to be a subject, of investigating the effects that such a notion has on our relationship to ourselves and others, and of exploring possible ways of thinking and acting differently" (Taylor 2011: 180).

Returning to Bauman, however, it would seem questionable as to whether the possibilities open to us in the contemporary world allow us the opportunity for such reflection. In a more recent interpretation of the postmodern condition, for instance, Bauman deploys the gardener and the hunter as opposing metaphors. And, whereas the gardener tends her/his plot with hope into the future, a utopia based on a better tomorrow, the hunter – Bauman's choice to represent today's world – lives for today. We exist then in a utopia of the present, in which, just like hunters, we are constantly on the move and, what is more, in a state of **permanent competition** with one another. Tellingly, this leaves us **no time for reflection**; where fashion takes the place of any deeper thoughts in relation to life and our place in it:

> Forming a life path of a never ending series of egotistical actions, arising from the next episode of the TV serial that is experienced, never giving us occasion to stop and think about the direction or sense of our life as it is. And when such an occasion does eventually arise, that is, when we fall from or withdraw from the hunter way of life, it is generally already too late for reflection to have any influence on the shape of our life and those around us. Too late for a life shaped in opposition to the "existing reality", and particularly, a questioning as to its sense that would bring any practical benefits. (Bauman 2011: 45, translation – MB)

Further to this, and perhaps in acknowledgment of its drastic implications, Michał Zawadzki (2009: 6, translation – MB) sums up the contemporary situation as one which actually threatens the human condition, where the move towards "individualization [...] has made uncertainty the foundation of individual biographies [...] [something which] influences people's conduct, attitudes and values, as well as their lifestyles." This element of uncertainty invading past, present and future, to the extent that what were previously taken to be "unshakable" rules, values and norms, are now disintegrating. As Zawadzki (2009: 6–7, translation – MB) writes further:

> Traditional family ties and also ties of a religious character – the regulatory bases of individual biographies –have been put in doubt. This atrophy has also affected values connected with everyday experience and the ties between people – which have taken on an episodic and fleeting character, resulting in provisional social relations, [...] [where] carnival has become the normal run of life

and where the old and accepted authorities no longer apply. And, as Mikhail Bakhtin (1984: 256) writes, "Carnival with all its images, indecencies, and curses affirms the people's immortal, indestructible character. In the world of carnival the awareness of the people's immortality is combined with the realization that established authority and truth are relative".

1.2. Education, schooling and the world at large

That there is awareness of culture having an effect on education cannot be doubted. At the international level, an influential report by UNECSO, drawn up by Jacques Delors and his team (Delors et al 1996), outlined what type of world the twenty-first century would be, as well as giving a response for education to that world, in the form of "four pillars" of education.

The report sums up the situation at the end of the twentieth century, moving into the twenty-first, as one in which technological advances have been made, along with a rise in living standards (although not shared equally by all people and in all countries). However, it also sees that there is growing disillusionment stemming from rising unemployment and exclusion in the developed world, as well as continuing inequalities in development in the world as a whole (Delors et al 1996: 13). In addition, it perceives the challenges facing the world into the future as those of sustainable development, the new forms of international cooperation that will develop as well as the need to embrace scientific and technological development and the changes in culture and adaptation in terms of people's mentalities this will bring. In achieving the latter, it sees the issues underlying educational policy in the twenty-first century as a number of "tensions" to be confronted and overcome. And it is in these tensions, it seems to me, that there is acknowledgement of the fragmentary and conflictual nature of present-day existence as outlined above. These tensions are between the global and the local, the universal and the individual, tradition and modernity, long-term and short-term considerations, the need for competition and the concern for the equality of opportunity, the extraordinary expansion of knowledge and the capacity of human beings to assimilate it, and the spiritual and the material (Delors et al 1996: 16). Further to this, in helping to create this better world and alleviate the tensions that are listed, the report suggests that education in the twenty-first century needs to be underpinned by **four essential concepts**, which it calls **pillars**. These are *learning to live together*, *learning to know*, *learning to do* and *learning to be*.

Learning to live together is the development of a shared understanding of other people, including their traditions, history and spiritual beliefs. This, in turn, if it is to be fulfilled, will also involve acknowledgement of a world of growing interdependence, where common projects need to be encouraged and carried out. *Learning to know*, is the pursuit of education throughout the whole of one's life, which, because of the rapid changes taking place in the world, must be broad enough to allow people to engage with education when it is needed, and specific enough to deal with subjects useful in the tackling of particular projects. *Learning to do* concerns our ability to do a particular job of work but also cope with many different situations, both foreseen and unforeseen. It also emphasizes teamwork as an essential strategy and the promotion of hands on experience. The final of the four pillars, *learning to be*, is, as the report announces, the tapping of the internal resources that everyone has (to offer), such as "memory, reasoning power, imagination, physical ability, aesthetic sense, the aptitude to communicate with others and the natural charisma of the group leader" (Delors et al 1996: 21), and which should help facilitate the growth of independence and self-judgement in people as well as feelings of personal responsibility when it comes to fulfilling their own and shared aims.

Importantly, in implementing these pillars, Delors and the team reaffirm the place of the formal education system, although not without placing demands upon teachers and the system itself. For teachers especially, the report underlines the authority they have and the **dialogical approach** that should be the basis for the relationship they form with pupils. It also (re)states their basic role as people involved in communicating knowledge about the whole of the world. In relation to this, learning should be about "the acquisition, renewal and use of knowledge" (Delors et al 1996: 22) as well as, in the information age, the provision of skills allowing for the selection, arrangement, management and use of information once it has been gathered. Importantly, it also emphasizes the correlation between the education system and society as a whole, and the need for the former to keep pace with the latter.

Indeed, in connection with this, as Jerome Bruner (1999: 43) so aptly states, education "is a complex pursuit of fitting a culture to the needs of its members and of fitting its members and their ways of knowing to the needs of the culture". And, in compiling an agenda for an education that is responsive to these needs, Bruner proposes **nine tenets** that should **underlie educational practice** and that will make it "culture active" rather than "culture passive". The tenets he gives relate to the following areas: perspective, constraint, constructivism, interaction; externalization; instrumentalism; institution; identity and self-esteem, and narrative (Bruner 1999: 13–43). Since these tenets include ideas and issues that touch upon my own ideas concerning happening in education, I will describe them below.

Generally, Bruner proposes that there needs to be an understanding from all those involved in education that meaning is constructed and that this construction takes place between people who are actively engaged in working together doing something. There is also an acknowledgment that in working together to produce something, a mutual identity is forged and reinforced, while the product which results from it, its "externalization", makes explicit cognitive activity which is usually implicit. According to Bruner, other positive aspects of this teamwork, which includes the teacher as a definite part of the team, is that it fosters tradition-inventing that includes learners in processes that occur equally in wider culture.

Bruner's (1999: 17) agenda also emphasizes the vital role that language should play in the educational enterprise, both as an image system and the means of providing the "toolkit" culture has developed to "empower human beings to go beyond their 'native' predispositions". This makes it possible, as Bruner (1999: 18) phrases it, to "stand on the shoulders of the giants who preceded us". In addition to this, all those involved in education (society as a whole) need to acknowledge that in its institutional form, it is politically situated, and that it has social and economic consequences away from its immediate surroundings, into the futures of its learners. Moreover, institutionalized education has an important role to play in preparing learners to take part in other institutions once they leave school, as it prepares them to cope with the array of symbolic apparatuses that function throughout all institutions, as well as the fact that they work on the basis of coercion and voluntarism, competition, privilege and power.

Continuing with Bruner's nine tenets for an education that would be culture responsive, he also posits identity and self-esteem, as well as narrative, as factors that have important roles to play. With reference to the former, Bruner (1999: 35) writes: "Perhaps the single most universal thing about human experience is the phenomenon of 'Self', and we know that education is crucial to its formation". The self that should be involved in education is, moreover, one that has agency, so that it can start and complete activities on its own, as well as evaluate its effectiveness in doing so. And here, Seymour Epstein's (2003: 160–161) cognitive-experiential self-theory (CEST) provides an explanation of how the subject builds both a theory of the reality that surrounds her/him, as well as the self, using mutually supportive rational and experiential information processing systems: the former being a system that adapts by learning through experience, the latter, through logical inference. This is a concept which also has implications for education in that it stresses the need for experience as an important factor in learning; that is, in the subject's construction of her/his world and self, and not just one based on rational analysis and thinking.[5] Additionally, Kazimierz Dąbrowski's (1988: 43–44) theory of positive disintegration provides an explanation of how the subject is able to move to a higher level of awareness through the disintegration of a less aware self, which demands that the subject (in this case the learner) is conscious of and engaged in the processes with which she/he is occupied.

According to Bruner too, as part and parcel of the agency mentioned above, school must not forget that it has a nurturing role to play, so that a pupil's personal development, in terms of self-esteem, also needs to be part of the educational picture and not only the fulfilling of performance criteria. This recognition of an area of affective influence also relates back to Epstein's (2003: 161) rational processing system, which, as the author states, is emotionally driven, as "affect determines what is attended to and reinforced, without affect there would be neither schemas nor motivation in the experiential system, and, therefore, no experiential system". This, in turn, would result in the impoverishment or non-existence of interpersonal relations, creativity and empathy, all of which are linked to the experiential system.

Bruner's (1999: 39–42) last idea for culture in education concerns **narrative**, which again features as one of the important factors in Epstein's (2003: 160) experiential system, as a way of encoding reality. For Bruner too, narrative is the ability of learners (all people) to create *their* version of *their* world. In terms of education especially, this means allowing self-generated discovery through which learners can find themselves in a subject (rather than having it imposed upon them). This narrative thinking rather than logical-scientific thinking, so Bruner believes, has been somewhat neglected in education, even though, according to

5 Indeed, Epstein posits that we could in fact exist without the rational system, whereas life without the experiential would be untenable.

Trzebiński (2002), it is central to the way we live and understand life. It is also something that is not simply "given" but needs to be worked on and cultivated. All the more reason then, to view narrative as something essential to the educational enterprise, especially since, as Bruner describes, the world is such a complex and complicated place and where there are so many narratives to be had, some of them perhaps less desirable than others:

> Feeling at home in the world, knowing how to place oneself into self-descriptive stories, is surely not made easier by the enormous increase in migration in the modern world. It is not easy, however multicultural your intentions, to help a ten-year-old create a story that includes him in the world beyond his family and neighborhood, having been transplanted from Vietnam to the San Fernando Valley, from Algeria to Lyons, from Anatolia to Dresden. If school, his *pied-à-terre* outside the family, can't help him, there are alienated countercultures that can. (Bruner 1999: 41)

In this concern, there would appear to be an implicit reference to the descriptions of the fragmented world given at the very beginning of this chapter, while Bruner's final comments on narrative and the central role it has to play in education, and through that the fixing of ourselves in the world as a whole, return us to the idea that culture and education are inseparably intertwined:

> A system of education must help those growing up in a culture find an identity within that culture. Without it, they stumble in their effort after meaning. It is only in the narrative mode that one can construct an identity and find a place in one's culture. Schools must cultivate it, nurture it, cease taking it for granted. (Bruner 1999: 42)

Dorota Klus-Stańska, working within the Polish context, also links this larger cultural context to school education and, in particular, emphasizes the need for changes in education to parallel those taking place in society. Klus-Stańska (2002: 390, translation – MB) observes: "School always functions in relation to culture. It grows from it and has an important role in ensuring its continuation", although there may come a time when school must undergo certain changes because of changes in society itself. Klus-Stańska (2002: 390, translation – MB) writes further:

> Things become complicated when there are changes in culture which are so violent that school, as a bureaucratic structure, needs to respond to them, without waiting for the next generation of teachers to usher in the new climate. In the meantime, a situation may arise where school which, up until this point, has fulfilled its task well, adequate to the wider cultural, demographic, societal and political context, fails to keep up with the changes. In such a case, a modification of the overall functioning of schools is necessary, where learners must be made ready to participate in a culture that is changing, able to understand it and define their place within it.

Here therefore, it is not the case that **school** is bad or negative but simply that it is **not adequate in relation to the changes taking place in society**.

The situation, however, is perhaps not as easily settled as creating a more adequate and responsive educational system. As Eugenia Potulicka and Joanna Rutkowiak (2012) highlight, changes in society itself might, in fact, hinder the development of such a system. This is because acquiescence to one particular viewpoint in relation to running the system might prove detrimental to it; especially when it comes to learners understanding as fully as possible the culture they belong to and their place within it.

Rutkowiak, for example, criticizes the neoliberal colonization of the schooling agenda which has taken place almost worldwide (including Poland) over the past thirty years. For the author, its economic imperative is especially harmful, as it touches upon everything, from the way that schools are funded, via the shape in which choice is presented, the form and content of lessons, to the manner in which pupils are assessed, all of which have a circular, "self-fulfilling" impact on pupils, teachers and schools alike (Rutkowiak 2012: 22–27). Most unsettling is the mode in which she sees learners being indoctrinated into a system of consumption and consumerism where the underlying rule is: "I HAVE THEREFORE I AM, AND I AM THAT WHICH I HAVE; THEREFORE, THE MORE I HAVE, THE MORE I AM" (Rutkowiak 2012: 18, translation – MB).[6] The schooling which promotes this being one in which there is

> A weakening of the interpretation and critical penetration of phenomena [...] [because in] the reality of consumption the a-reflexive individual is necessary, one who does not discern the negative aspects of his own dichotomization, and for whom even help is simplified, because she/he is not trained to think, it tires her/him. (Rutkowiak 2012: 24, translation – MB)

Interestingly enough, there is an awareness in Delors' report that **education is hard pressed by economic and financial arguments**. Arguments, moreover, which do not make a priority of the fact that "education has a fundamental role to play in personal and social development" (Delors et al 1996: 9), especially in its critical aspect. This is perhaps even more so nowadays when the intensification of a neoliberal agenda with regard to all sectors of society (including education), *in spite of* the recent financial crisis, continues to have a marked effect. A more recent report from UNESCO relating to education into the future (Narayan 2012) acknowledges the role of the concept of the pillars of lifelong learning in lifting the worldwide educational agenda beyond simply functional literacy (Narayan

6 Original in capital letters.

2012: 16), although it also recognizes that the world today is very different to what it was twenty years ago (Narayan 2012: 14). And, while generally the chief concerns remain the same: sustainable growth, global cooperation, closing gaps in disparity as well as inclusiveness, there are changes which place the consideration of economic factors much more centrally. Connected to this, economic growth is also seen as a priority for societies across the world, with education being seen, first and foremost, as facilitating that growth (Narayan 2012: 14).

This placement of economic markers much more centrally again comes with a warning for education: that concentrating on outcomes as a mark of success should not divert from quality of input and, on from this, the learning that takes place (Narayan 2012: 17). In this particularly, there is an echo of a concern that Rutkowiak (2012: 23) raises in terms of the neoliberalization of the educational debate: where assessment of the whole is reliant upon end results, *product*, to the ignorance of, or, indeed, detriment to engagement in any of the valuable *processes* that exist.

1.3. The demands on education and schooling

In relation to what has been outlined above and in the perceived need to support the development of citizens who can fully partake in the contemporary world, "Politicians at European level have recognized that education and training are essential to the development and success of today's knowledge society and economy" (*European Union Policy Document Key Competences for Schooling* 2009). Acknowledgement of this has been translated into the *European Union's Key Competences for Schooling*. In the introduction, it states: "In an increasingly complex world, creativity, the ability to think laterally, transversal skills and adaptability will be valued more than the specific bodies of knowledge that schools have traditionally dispensed" (*European Union's Key Competences for Schooling* 2009). This being the case, and looking at the overall aims for the **curricula for the different cycles of Polish schooling**, the competences outlined above can clearly be seen in a number of important attributes that the recently reformed education system wants to propagate.

In the general introductions to the various curricula that form the basis for Polish compulsory education,[7] Zbigniew Marciniak, like Bruner, links school

7 Each of the curricula is contained in a separate volume and each volume starts with a general introduction by Marciniak. These introductions are basically the same with minor changes relating to the specific needs of the level or subject area. The volume I refer to is number 7, the one prepared for art and culture.

and the outside world. He also comments on the need for reform as a result of pressure from that world. An important element Marciniak mentions in this respect is a European initiative, the Bolonia process, which is part of an attempt to make education more accessible to a greater number of people at higher levels and across borders, which, in turn, has had an impact on primary and secondary levels of education. This, of course, comes back to the explicit aims of the European Union mentioned above, which sees successful economic development in terms of having a population that is well educated. Another factor driving reform in Poland has, however, been internal: to make the system more relevant to the needs of the learners using it. In effect, to take greater advantage of the six years of general education following the primary cycle: to create a sense of development for those taking part, rather than the repetition and stagnation that are felt to underlie the system at present. In writing about this, Marciniak (2013: 9, translation – MB) sees the possibilities opened up during this period as allowing learners to gain "a joint and solid foundation of general knowledge, after which every learner significantly deepens that knowledge in areas that are suitable to their individual interests and predispositions".

In a way here, Marciniak appears to be trying to **balance the more traditional role of school** as **a provider of knowledge** with the **more contemporary demands** being placed upon it which are expressed in the European Union's key competences given above. It should come as no surprise then that as well as reiterating the need for sound foundations in terms of knowledge in each of the different subject areas, the curricula for Polish primary and secondary education also place emphasis on developing learner competences that are not subject orientated but rather skills orientated. In one particular passage in the curricula, a *leitmotif* for both primary and secondary cycles,[8] Marciniak (2013: 21, translation – MB) expresses the European Union competences in the following way:

> In the process of general education, [...] school teaches pupils the basic skills to support their further development both individual and social, those skills such as: [...] cognitive interest, creativity, [...] readiness to participate in culture, to take the initiative as well as to be involved in group work.

Throughout the text these points are also further emphasized when, for example, mention is made of helping younger learners develop in relation to their own abilities (Marciniak 2013: 17), or that they should be given the possibilities to satisfy their curiosity and find out what they are interested in for their present

8 I am quoting from the secondary sector curriculum although the wording remains the same for the primary sector.

and future development (Marciniak 2013: 15), as well as being given help to prepare them to function within the contemporary world. For older learners, in addition to selecting information and critically analyzing it (Marciniak 2013: 19), it also means the ability to take important decisions (Marciniak 2013: 22).

It should be stressed, however, that even though Bruner and Marciniak share an interest in promoting development in the learner that is not simply subject based, but relating to the "Self", their starting points for such promotion are not the same. Whereas Bruner has a viewpoint which is anthropological, placing people at the centre of the educational process, Marciniak's is bureaucratic, where the functioning of education, after Bogusław Śliwerski (2009: 136), can be seen as a mechanism; one, moreover, which runs the risk of losing sight of the people working within it, concentrating simply on the correct functioning of procedures.[9] In addition to this, with regard to the Polish curricula, Marciniak's seriousness of intent to foster skills important to the development of the "Self" of learners, can be judged by the fact that in programme documents that run to more than seventy pages, approximately thirty lines are devoted to these skills, with no mention as to how they might actually be promoted.

1.4. Alternatives in education

There are, of course, a number of ways in which the above mentioned forms of engagement might be encouraged in schools: moving the school on from its more traditional role of providing information and knowledge to one in which learners are actively involved in finding out for themselves, developing skills that will be useful and applicable throughout their lives beyond school and not simply within it. As we have seen above, Bruner's nine tenets are an attempt to provide concepts and practices for education that will be open to the wider world, engage the learner and be supportive of her/his growth. In a very real sense, the debate around alternatives in education, as well as the proposals it has to offer, is also about this. It is therefore interesting to see the issues that are focused upon in two recent Polish academic post-conference publications in which various

9 In connection with this too, it is interesting to note what Śliwerski has written about the situation in which a set of ideas or procedures are given from above, as objectives to be implemented. There is little chance that this will occur, as the people responsible for the implementation will do everything they can to block it if they feel it is against their interests (Śliwerski 2009: 324). Or, if it is implemented, it is done so in a desultory way where there is little or no feeling of responsibility for what is occurring (Śliwerski 2009: 136).

alternatives are explored. Each publication, among other issues, debates how to place learners more centrally in the educational experience, and make education itself – school – more responsive to learner needs and the world to which it belongs.

In one of the publications, concerning the alternatives open to education at present (Śliwerski 2010), three areas are considered:

(1) different models and practices of education,
(2) the conditions under which they (as alternatives) exist,
(3) inquiries into educational and social alternatives.

In relation to the first area, for example, New Education pedagogies from the previous century such as Deweyesque schooling and the Warldorf method are reviewed alongside other educational practices at different levels, and from different countries around the world, such as preschool in Italy, lower-secondary in Norway and university in North America. In the second area, there is coverage of the social issues that have an impact on education, with articles that present a possibility for identity in today's world, how youngsters view future society, and the gap between society's ideas of political correctness and the reality that actually exists. In the third area, meanwhile, various inquiries into alternative models of schooling and lifestyles are included. With the former this includes the use of new technology with young learners or learners with special needs, with the latter, homosexuality and cohabitation as alternatives to existing lifestyle models.

In the second publication (Hurło, Klus-Stańska and Łojko 2009), there are examinations of issues that underlie the possibilities for alternatives in education at a paradigmatic level. The debate, in this particular case, is also presented across three areas:

(1) the prevailing theoretical, ideological and political discourses perceived to influence didactics;
(2) the learner, knowledge and education in general;
(3) the influence of adults and the "outside world".

In the first instance, the situation of didactics and education overall is reviewed, including sociological and ideological concerns, didactics in relation to a number of subject disciplines and issues (special needs, gender equality), and the role / influence of different "-isms" (objectivism; constructivism; reconstructivism) within didactics. With the second area of debate, various types and levels of schooling as well as subject areas are considered, in addition to the needs of learners, and the ways learners are stereotyped in particular subject areas. In the third area, meanwhile, and in relation to school education in particular, different aspects relating to teachers, their competencies and relations with learners as well as external factors, such as the current economic situation, are investigated.

This shows the **rich** and **vibrant landscape of exploration for alternatives in education** (in Poland) that exists at the present time. A landscape that, as Czesław Kupisiewicz (2010: 23, translation – MB) would have it, seeks to

> be OPEN to that which surrounds it, for that which is innovatory and creative, which stimulates learners to independent thinking and action, to their own form of cognition, which makes them interested, stimulates group work, both in thought and manually

and thereby, it might be added, also helps learners to become flexible, not only in their thinking and practices of thinking, but also in their relations with others and how they might work together. Indeed, the situation is summed up succinctly by Kupisiewicz (2010: 23, translation – MB) when he states that "for learners it is life and not just preparation for it": a life, moreover, that, as was outlined at the beginning of this chapter, is extremely dynamic.

To this varied collection of ideas and practices as to how learner engagement and development might be encouraged and helped, I would like to add a consideration of happening.

1.5. Happening

My interest in the possibilities of using happening in an educational setting is not without its personal reasons. I completed my studies in the visual arts and have been involved in making happenings as an arts practitioner for over twenty years, during which time I have been interested in the type of participation it promotes. I am also a trained and practising English teacher with an interest in the performative aspects of that profession. Over the years, involvement in both these practices has led to a certain amount of cross-feed between the two, so that elements of happening have found their way into my teaching and vice-versa. In this situation, it appears "quite obvious" that happening does have something to offer education in relation to the stated aims of the European Union and the curricula mentioned above (section 1.4), in that it creates opportunities to think laterally, develops transversal skills and calls upon participants to be adaptable.

Dictionary definitions of happening would appear to support this. One such definition describes happening as something "organized and directed [...] whose aim is to shock the public, to electrify their imagination with an unexpected presentation of facts" (Słownik-online 2005). Another dictionary goes on to say it is "an essentially unrepeatable event or series of events designed to evoke a spontaneous audience reaction to sensory, emotional, or spiritual stimuli", with additional information relating to its form, that it is "usually [an] unscripted or improvised often multimedia public performance in which the audience participates" (Quirk 1991: 719). In both definitions, the idea given is of a practice that engages and mentally stimulates its audience in some way, so that it is apparent, even from these extremely limited descriptions, happening may have applications in education in relation to the cognitive (imagination), the variety of ways in which it presents and expects information to be received, as well as its participatory nature.

It is perhaps no surprise then that happening and what can be considered as its precursors have been linked to education. Allan Kaprow (Kelly 2003: 55), one of the founding fathers of the form, sees the job of the artist as essentially an educational one,

> to place at the disposal of a receptive audience those new thoughts, new words, new stances even, that will enable their work to be better understood. If they do not, the public's alternative is its old thoughts and attitudes, loaded with stereotypical hostilities and misunderstandings.

He also sees "the experimental arts" (and here we can place happening-type activities) as growing out of models of communication to be found in society itself. One of these is learning models, which include "(allegories of philosophical inquiry, sensitivity-training rituals, and educational demonstrations)" (Kelly 2003: 130). Moreover, Kaprow (Kelly 2003: 165) described one of his fellow happener's enactments[10] as "a consciousness-raising device, as teaching, as behaviour changing". In commenting on the script for his happening *Gayety*, meanwhile, Claes Oldenburg writes about wanting to create what would amount to a personal, civic report on the community of Chicago; the aim being, one might assume, to describe and, through that, understand that community better (Kirby 1966: 234–235). There also appears to be an educational agenda at the heart of Tadeusz Kantor's involvement in art as a whole. For the Polish artist, "The conflict brought about by creativity is the source and motive of movement, change and development" (Borowski 1982: 8, translation – MB). Meanwhile, Jerzy Bereś sees his activities[11] as dealing with social matters; their enactment being a dialogue with reality and a provocation that is meant to inspire participants (Bereś, Kasprzycki and Łubowski 2009: 58–59).

---

10 Wolf Vostell's *Berlin Fever* (1976).

11 The output of Bereś has been described in various ways: "actions", "masses", "prophecies" or "manifestations".

Additionally, if the meaning of education is understood in its broadest sense as a process which "has an influence on the psyche and behavior of people" (Rubacha 2007a: 59) and which may include the imparting of knowledge and development of the person or persons involved in that process, then happening, along with its antecedents and the performance art that followed it, might be said to be, to a lesser or greater extent, educational. In some cases, this educational aim is made explicit, as with the short-lived and none too successful Dada classes held in Zurich (Goldberg 1990: 65–66), the performance classes at the Bauhaus (Goldberg 1990: 102–104), or contemporary performance art and, more precisely, the pedagogy that has sprung up from this, performance art pedagogy (Garoian 1999). In other cases, this educational aim is more covert, hidden under the seemingly ranting and free-ranging polemic of manifesto, as with the Italian Futurists (Harrison and Wood 1994: 145–149), or the agit-prop of the Russian Futurists (Harrison and Wood 1994: 308) and Constructivists (Harrison and Wood 1994: 317–318) in the years following the Russian Revolution. In addition to and related to this, it is also possible to describe the position each of these performance arts adopts in terms of its educational purposes: political, aesthetic and institutional, or a mixture of all three, which is invariably the case.

1.6. Concluding remarks

The world is fragmented and changing, a place where traditional authorities and certainties no longer apply and where there are difficulties to establish one's identity as well as one's place within society. In such a situation, there is a need for education to be more involved with society, to help people prepare to live in the world. Meanwhile, as a way of achieving this aim, schooling needs to move on from its more traditional role of providing information and knowledge to one in which learners are actively involved in finding out things for themselves, developing skills that will be useful and applicable throughout the whole of their lives. With regard to this, happening would appear to be an appropriate practice for education to adopt.

In the following chapter, an attempt is made to gather together a number of ideas and terms relating to happening which can then be used when considering it in connection with education: in this way to construct a picture of happening in education based upon what happening actually is and what it has to offer.

2. A definition for happening

In Chapter 2, as a first step to create a much fuller picture of happening, an attempt is made to outline its characteristics. This involves a consideration of its roots in the visual arts, its connections to theatre, as well as, or perhaps above all, the difficulties in trying to encapsulate what happening is in a "once-and-for-all" (finite) definition. In addition to this, happening as a postmodern practice will be discussed. In the final part of the chapter, ideas of space and place are also looked at, before the presentation of a model of the limen as a possible operating space for happening.

From the outset it must be stated that happening has a complex and contradictory pedigree. Some practitioners and theoreticians view it as **an art form** based within the visual arts, whilst others view it as **a form of theatre**. Yet others believe that to develop it must look away from the visual arts for its inspiration and look towards **"real life"**. It is also seen by some commentators to be part of the modernist enterprise, while it is also possible to see it as part of the postmodern project, still being used by artists (and not only artists) up into the present time. Happening's complex lineage will now be looked at to try and gain a better understanding of its functioning and to define some salient characteristics, both of which will prove useful when considering a role for happening within education.

2.1. Happening as visual art, happening as theatre

Happening is a form that can be said to have its roots in the visual arts (Harrison and Wood 1994: 703–706, Goldberg 1990: 128). In this context, happenings first appeared in late 1950s America and continued to be popular, spreading to Europe and Japan, into the early 1970s. A **multidisciplinary** form, it grew out of dissatisfaction with existing art and performance practices, which were seen to be inadequate in their engagement with audiences and the world in general. A result of this opening up of art and what it entailed aesthetically is perhaps best conveyed by Grzegorz Dziamski when he writes about happening and its related practices. His difficulty in trying to pin down such amorphous art forms is also hinted at when Dziamski chooses to place them together more by what they negate rather than share:

> In the last forty years, action art, happening, actions and performances have formed a new artistic field which does not belong to either the theatre or the plastic arts, and what is more, destroys the concept and classification formed in the eighteenth century,

> of the so called fine arts (beaux arts), reaching for such para-artistic forms as circus acts, street parades, jugglers and conjurors at fairs, church parades, carnival processions and games, firework displays, cabaret jokes, gags, light and sound projections and so on [...]. Art has stopped being the main point of reference for these activities; while the meaning of a number of these presentations must be examined in the light of a broader, general cultural context, as the individual's story about her/his own world. (Dziamski 1997: 367, translation – MB)

Concentrating more fully on happenings, the variety of possibilities open to it as an art form is perhaps most readily seen in the coinage of different names by a number of practitioners to describe what are effectively happenings. Bereś (Bereś, Kasprzycki and Łubowski 2009: 59), for example, has named his *not* happenings "Visions", "Altars", "Manifestations" and "Transfigurations", while Kaprow, who is considered by some to be the father of happening,[12] also used the names "actions", "events" and "activities" (Garoian 1999: 50).

In addition to this, and bringing the situation up-to-date, a contemporary Polish theatre group which has produced happenings, *Teatr Strefa Ciszy*, labels its performances in various ways: "street action", "theatre action", "special project" or "theatre event", a number of which originally started out as happenings (Tyszka 2003: 129–133). As well as this rich terminology used by the practitioners themselves, more general and inclusive terms have also been applied to happening as it has continued to evolve. As a result of this, now it is more likely to be subsumed under the heading of performance art or live art (Herbert 1994: 31), or to be seen as part of the history of devising, a creative strategy open to performers of all kinds (Heddon and Milling 2006: 63–94).

At this point, it is also worth mentioning the differences between happenings from the 1960s that Stefan Morawski (1971a: 114) outlines, relating to particular happeners and their countries of origin. For Morawski, the American happeners, such as Kaprow and Oldenburg, were concerned with the material world and the surfeit of goods that surrounded them, bound to their situation of belonging to an affluent society; although their activities were not critical but rather accepting of the situation in which they found themselves. The happenings of the French happener, Jean-Jacques Lebel, meanwhile, had a social-political character, connected with various aspects of life in general, of which, as Morawski writes, he was totally critical. Wolf Vostell, coming from the then West Germany, had happenings of a similar character to Lebel's, with the difference that they created

12 This attribution has recently been in dispute. For a brief outline of the situation as it stands, see Heddon and Milling (2006: 67).

situations where participants might break with everyday life and thereby gain distance to themselves and become aware of the conventions of life which surrounded them.

Describing the "creative enterprise" of happening in more detail, the complex nature of the form becomes apparent. In what amounts to a personal manifesto in relation to happening, Kaprow (Harrison and Wood 1994: 706) wrote that "the source of themes, materials, actions, and the relationships between them are to be derived from any place or period except from the arts, their derivatives, and their milieu". This denial of art being presupposed on the proposition that "The line between art and life should be kept as fluid, and perhaps indistinct, as possible", and this is not because the arts are "bad", but rather because "they contain highly sophisticated habits" which, if avoided, might lead to a situation where "a new language will develop that has its own standards". In a description from 1966, Kaprow actually enumerates the practices happening has affinities with and which are marginal to the fine arts:

> parades, carnivals, games, expeditions, guided tours, orgies, religious ceremonies, and such secular rituals as the elaborate operations of the Mafia; civil rights demonstrations; national election campaigns; Thursday nights at the shopping centers of America; the hot-rod, dragster, and motorcycle scene; and, not least, the whole fantastic explosion of the advertizing and communications industry. Each of these plays with the materials of the tangible world, and the results are partly conscious ceremonies acted out from day to day. Happenings, freed from the restrictions of conventional art materials, have discovered the world at their fingertips, and the intentional results are quasi-rituals never to be repeated. […] Happenings do not merely allude to what is going on in our bedrooms, in the drugstores, and at the airports; they are right there. (Kelly 2003: 64–65)

However, in what appears to be a contradictory amendment to this anti-art stance, Kaprow then adds "Happening is conceived as an art, certainly, but this is for lack of a better word, or one that would not cause endless discussion". Happening then is not art, but it is *an* art.

To find out what Kaprow might actually mean by this, it is probably best to turn to another artist, Vostell, and his statement about happening. This captures the idea of a similar shift of art into life, one, however, where such a movement places the participant firmly in a present reality – "here and now" – where everything is called into question:

> happening = life – life as art – no retreat from but *into* reality – making it possible to experience and live its essence – not to abandon the world but to find a new relation to it – to let the participant experience himself consciously in the happening – to shift the environment into new contexts – to create new meanings by breaking up the old – let the participant experience indeterminacy as a creative force – to uncover and let uncover

> nonsense in sense – lack of purpose as purpose – open form as form – eccentricity – participants and performers instead of spectators – simultaneousness through juxtaposition of contradictory elements – new combination and absurd use of everyday objects. (Heddon and Milling 2006: 66)

There is also an implication here of a new role for people involved in such an activity. They become **participants** who work alongside performers in uncovering the world. This **move from a passive to an active involvement**, whereby the audience works with the performers, is seen by Deirdre Heddon and Jane Milling (2006: 66) as a "sign of the times", in line with a particular period in history when participatory democracy was being called for. This democratizing impulse can also be seen at the aesthetic level, where happening is inclusive of many different forms of expression and communication, rather than being confined to one accepted and acceptable form. Such a spirit on the aesthetic level is also very much present in the ideas underlying Kaprow's practice. The artist was strongly influenced by Dewey's *Art as Experience*, within which the philosopher, in a number of complex and interconnecting considerations, tries to link artistic aesthetic concerns back to those of everyday life, calling for an art that was closer to the ordinary experiences of the majority of people if it was to have any sense or be appreciated (Dewey 1958: 3–6). With his happenings, in part, Kaprow also set out to achieve this aim.

In seeming contravention of this "anti-art strand", but very much under the happening banner, Kantor created performances that he always maintained were art, and not only that, in at least three examples of his happenings there are overt references to the work of other artists: Durer, Rembrandt and Gericault.[13] This might seem to call into question Kantor's claim to be a creator of happenings. However, it is perhaps more relevant to see it in terms of the artist's adopted position in relation to contemporary art practice and art in general, as well as to his own creative process. As Jarosław Suchan (2000: 95–96) claims, Kantor adopted a heretical stance towards all forms of convention, disliking any attempts to restrain art within existing patterns. As a result of this, his choice of a particular form was, at one and the same time, a use of that form to communicate a particular message, as well as being a question to the form itself. This being the case, the concentration of consciousness and awareness that Vostell brings to everyday life through the creation of happening is additionally utilized by Kantor to turn a critical eye on the rules and norms that are seen to be part of the practice of happening itself.

13 Durer – *A Meeting with the Rhinoceros of Durer* (1968), Rembrandt – *The Anatomy Class According to Rembrandt* (1969), and Gericault – *Medusa's Raft*, as part of Panoramic Sea Happening (1967).

Suchan gives a number of examples. For the purposes of Kantor's happenings, for instance, paintings do not function as works of art but as *ready-mades*, to be entered into dialogue with and exploited by the artist during the performance, very much as an object might be. In addition to this, participation in happening, where audience and performers work together, is replaced by a form of involvement where the audience are told what to do by Kantor, a situation which leads Suchan to believe the true aim here was not to promote a more active and egalitarian working relationship between artist and audience but rather to examine the nature of the participation itself (Suchan 2000: 99).[14] Because of this, there is at one and the same time an emancipatory and critical edge to Kantor's work as a happener.

As well as the references to art and the form of participation, both of which appear to contradict happening practice, Suchan also suggests that Kantor called into question the "here and now" of happening. For example, in the *Panoramiczny happening morski* (Panoramic Sea Happening), by posing his audience-participants like the characters from Gericault's painting, *The Raft of Medusa*, a reference is made to an artwork produced a century earlier about a contemporary event. It was also something that occurred on the high seas and to a French sailing vessel, therefore, a location many miles from the Polish seaside resort where the happening took place and from a different nation's history. In this particular part of the happening then, "here and now" is replaced by "then and there". The whole experience is also further complicated by the fact that the participants in the *Medusa* section of the happening did not get dressed up or try to replicate the painting more fully. Neither was the raft meant to be identical to the one shown on canvas. And, in this, as Suchan proposes, Kantor is once again able to create a dissonance between our expectations and the norms of the particular art form in which he is working: the sea, the raft and the poses of the participants point to an art reference which places us in another time and place; while the fact that the people are dressed as themselves, holidaymakers on a beach, brings us back to the seaside resort of Osieki.

---

14 The idea that happeners generally took a more controlling role in their happenings has recently been confirmed by Oldenburg who, along with Kaprow, was one of the first happeners in the United States. In talking about his own happenings he comments: "Well I was definitely the director. [...] I was definitely violating the laws of the happening, let's say that. The idea that they sprang out of casual and chance things just wasn't true. They were organized. The only thing was that they were organized very quickly" (Ayres 2012).

This dissonance relating to form and content is not only restricted to Kantor "playing" with the conventions of happening, but rather, I would suggest, one of happening's characteristics generally, where there is dislocation between what is viewed or experienced and the interpretations made. This opens up the possibility of seeing both form and content from different and unexpected perspectives, where form itself has content. A situation which has greater implications than simply the aesthetic, for as Włodzimierz Pawluczuk (1978b: 88–89) has written, such an interplay, where a person has distance to form, is vital for psychological development, both of the self and in relation to others, as well as holding transformative possibilities (Pawluczuk 1978a: 107–108).

If the attributes of happening presented above are to be found in an area between art and life, and back again, yet another commentator, Michael Kirby (1966: 11), links happening directly to the theatre when he states:

> Although some of their advocates claim they are not, Happenings, like musicals and plays, are a form of theatre. Happenings are **a new form of theatre** [my emphasis – MB], just as collage is a new form of visual art, and they can be created in various styles just as collages (and plays) are.

And indeed, if happening is looked at against one of the models of *theatre* that performance theorist Richard Schechner proposes,[15] then it does appear to belong to that tradition. Schechner's model comprises of drama, script, theatre and performance, with each of these parts conceptualized as circles resting one upon the other:

> *Drama:* the smallest, most intense (heated up) circle. A written text, score, scenario, instruction, plan, or map. The drama can be taken from place to place or time to time independent of the person or people who carry it.
>
> *Script:* all that can be transmitted from time to time and place to place; the basic code of the events. The script is transmitted person to person, the transmitter is not a mere messenger.
>
> *Theater:* the event enacted by a specific group of performers; what the performers actually do during production. […] Usually, the theater is the manifestation or representation of the drama and/or script.
>
> *Performance:* the broadest, most ill-defined disc. The whole constellation of events, most of them passing unnoticed, that take place in/among both performers and audience from the time the first spectator enters the field of the performance – the precinct where the theater takes place – to the time the last spectator leaves. (Schechner 1988: 72)

15 Schechner (1988: 68) prefers not to limit himself to the term "theatre", rather he calls it "The phenomena called either/all 'drama,' 'theater,' 'performance' ".

Looking at this general model and in relation to Kirby's (1966: 11–22) fuller description of happening as theatre, as well as other accounts,[16] happening *might* be described as theatre in that to varying levels and in various examples of the form, all of the above are to be found. However, on further analysis, and in relation to another model Schechner (1988: 120–124) proposes, the *efficacy-entertainment* braid, it becomes more difficult to place happening as purely theatre, that is as entertainment. Rather, and as Schechner (1988: 120) suggests, similar to most performance forms, happening finds itself on a continuum between *efficacy – ritual* (where "the performance's purpose is to effect transformations") and *entertainment – theater* (which is the commercial end of theatre and where, as the name suggests, the most important factor is to sell tickets and entertain people).

To gain an idea of what happening might be in terms of theatre which is not purely entertainment, two forms of theatre will now be looked at that can be placed at the *efficacy – ritual* end of the continuum and which, in a number of ways, may be seen to resemble happening in that they attempt to move closer to "life". The two theatres I will look at are Jerzy Grotowski's *Theatre Laboratory*,[17] and paratheatre, and Augusto Boal's *Theatre of the Oppressed*.

2.1.1. The efficacy theatres of Grotowski and Boal in relation to happening

2.1.1.1. Grotowski

Situating Grotowski's involvement in theatre as *efficacy – ritual* rather than *entertainment – theatre*, Osiński (2009: 12) is of the opinion that at all stages of his career Grotowski's work had a laboratory type character; that is the theatre director was initially interested in researching the nature of acting as fully as possible, with a view to finding out more about the activity itself. This initial inquiry then grew beyond purely theatrical concerns to encompass research into human existence as a whole, involving gatherings and activities that attempted to break

16 The statements, scripts from individual happeners as well as commentaries included in Kirby's volume are very illuminating on this point. Oldenburg in a recent interview with Ayres (2012) states outright that some happeners were involved in creating theatre.

17 A number of the descriptions given throughout Kolankiewicz's (1978) anthology of press reports and other writings give the impression of being about happenings; this is because of their participatory nature, the unexplained and not necessarily connected sequence of events, and the different senses involved. See, especially, participant descriptions of the "ule" (hives) (Kolankiewicz 1978: 50–51, 55–58).

free of the restrictions and conventions of everyday life[18] to reveal other, deeper aspects on the level of the philosophical (Kolankiewicz 1978: 110), psychological (p. 27), psycho-physical (p. 54), metaphysical (p. 62)[19] and spiritual (p. 59); or, in some cases, beyond any form of classification (p. 108), depending on the person's experience and her/his attempt to describe it in words.

Generally, by the mid 1960s, Grotowski was moving away from the idea of staging plays, concentrating first of all on actors and their craft, and then beyond that to the actors themselves, as people (Burzyński and Osiński 1978: 23). This resulted in a situation where ideas of the presentation and interpretation of a character were left behind, so that the actor now performed a human act, or as Grotowski would have it, a "total act". To attain this particular state, intensive training of the body was undertaken, the whole process being guided by the individual actors and the needs they perceived within themselves. These then were not improvisations or exercises with the aid of an instructor helping the actors to limber up in preparation for acting, but altogether a deeper process, one in which a greater risk was to be taken, where "It was necessary to encounter the unknown, the secrets to be uncovered in the active human being" (Burzyński and Osiński 1978: 36, translation – MB).

Meanwhile, the type of change Grotowski was expecting from participants of his paratheatre events is given in a description by Schechner (1988: 144–145):

> Much of the paratheatrical work involved invited participants working intensively, bringing about an intimacy and quasi-religious solidarity – "spontaneous communitas" – by means of exercises, group-encounter techniques, and the submission to the will of strong leaders. Grotowski's paratheatrical work has close analogies both to American encounter-group therapy and self-help weekends as well as traditional initiation rites where neophytes are separated from familiar surroundings, removed into liminal space (or liminoid) space and time where by means of ordeals they are "broken down".

Schechner (1988: 145) also hints at the danger of such an intensive approach which, because it lacked a final phase of reintegration, left all but the strongest of personalities disorientated, "hanging, betwixt and between".

---

18 A way also, perhaps, of freeing the actors from the restraints of disciplinary power that Foucault describes. A power through which the activities of the body are controlled "meticulously, exhaustively and continuously" (Hoffman 2011: 28).

19 In addition, Steven Weinstein relates the comical story of his attachment to a pair of boots that almost meant he failed to see the true significance of the "ul" in which he was involved (Kolankiewicz 1978: 75–76).

It is arguable if *all* the happeners felt the need to be so extreme in achieving their aims. Kaprow's (Goldberg 1990: 130) comment about his first happening that "the actions will mean nothing clearly formuable so far as the artist is concerned" seems too ambivalent to make such a determined course of action possible. However, as Tadeusz Pawłowski (1982: 8) writes, there were definitely social and psychological concerns evident in the happenings. It also becomes apparent that the different techniques and forms employed by happeners were seen to play an important part in achieving these concerns, as they "wished to change the given scheme of relations between people. Realizations of a psychotherapeutic character had the aim of freeing people from their subconscious complexes and inhibitions" (Pawłowski 1982: 8, translation – MB). The way that happeners used verbal but especially, non-verbal signals, also had a major role in this, so that "different varieties of exclamations, unconnected individual words and 'stream of consciousness' monologues without any ordered syntactical and semantic whole" (Pawłowski 1982: 36–37, translation – MB) were believed to reveal a person's subconscious interior, their complexes and what they were suppressing. And again, with the distance to their everyday lives such practices would give the participants in happening, it seems relevant here to refer back to Pawluczuk (section 2.1 above) and his ideas concerning distance to form and its importance to psychological development.

In addition to a similarity of purpose in relation to the individual as well as to the person on a social level, the happeners also share Grotowski's concern with the "here and now". For Grotowski, the very personal in-depth search realized in the "total act" is the moment when "the phenomenon of *hic et nunc* is achieved; it is neither a tale nor an illusion it is the present time" (Burzyński and Osiński 1978: 55, translation – MB). In the paratheatrical phase, too, an important part of the concept of the "here and now" was to create a situation in which people could meet together and "be themselves ('as they are') [...] becoming creative and spontaneous in commune with others" (Schechner 1988: 127). This shows similar concerns to Vostell in his description of happening given above (section 2.1), where he wants to "retreat *into* reality". In addition to this, as far as Leszek Kolankiewicz is concerned, Grotowski's "renewal" of community through the changes affected in the person also had a political dimension. For, as Kolankiewicz (1978: 16) notes, there was a democratization of culture at play in the paratheatrical events, where participants were actively involved with one another in the dramas of each other's lives, hoping for some form of transformation (Kolankiewicz 1978: 47–48) which might have lasting effect (p. 109). And with this, Heddon and Milling's comments about democracy bound up with the participatory aspirations of happening, also mentioned above (section 2.1), come to mind.

2.1.1.2. Boal

In addition to his own experimentation, Boal has worked through traditional theatrical practices established in Brazil to develop a series of theatrical forms in which members of the audience become active participants in the drama. This is achieved when they suggest changes to a given "script" or course of action, as well as taking part in what is actually being shown. As a result of this, theatre becomes "a practical vehicle for grass-roots activism" (Paterson cited in Bentley 2012) in which audience members are empowered to both imagine and enact change, which then impacts on their wider social situation.

The efficacy of Boal's theatre, therefore, lies in helping people towards a critical consciousness, allowing them "to question the nature of their historical and social situation – to read their world – with the goal of acting as subjects in the creation of a democratic society" (Bentley 2012). In this, Boal is closely linked to the emancipatory work of Paulo Freire, while, as with the Brazilian educator's pedagogy, Boal's theatre is community specific in that the theatre works with a particular group of people with definite needs to gain an understanding of their situation and the problems they face. As a result, the theatrical performance derives from the community and is created in interaction with actors of the theatre. There are also a number of forms to Boal's *Theatre of the Oppressed*, and these are worth outlining here to gain a better understanding of audience involvement.

In *Image Theatre*, for example, the protagonists show information about themselves through visualization – or, as Boal puts it, sculpting themselves and their fellow performers – so that information is given without using words. With *Invisible Theatre*, a scene is enacted by a number of the theatre's actors as if it were taking place for real, while *agent provocateur* actors mix with the general public and express different views upon what is occurring. The general public, meanwhile, are involved in the action without actually knowing it, so that "an unexpected subversion of 'normal' behaviour within that particular society" (Boal 1998: xx) takes place. In *Forum Theatre*, an incident or story from the participants own lives is staged, which they can interrupt at any given moment to suggest or act out alternatives, thereby changing the course of events. In this way, the audience become "spec-actors", active participants, in contrast to the more traditional "spectator", a passive receiver of what is given. These particular theatre forms are used to solve problems of a historical and social character, although Boal also extended his experimentation to include psycho-therapeutic work.

In relation to Boal's theatre demanding active involvement from its "audience", it shares similarities with happening, as well as with Grotowski's paratheatre.[20] There is also a sense in which Boal, through the use of theatre, wants to get to grips with the "here and now" of his audience and change their reality. In this, therefore, he shares Vostell's concern to show up the "absurdities" of the present situation whilst also creating a situation (through enactment) in which ideas for change are explored. There is, however, a difference in how they achieve this, and this is the way in which *Theatre of the Oppressed* embraces the tradition of theatre and happening does not.

Boal's theatre, first and foremost, is grounded in a deep knowledge of theatre and its practice, which is illustrated most clearly in the way in which he places *Theatre of the Oppressed* (Boal 1985) within a greater theatrical tradition, citing Aristotle, Machiavelli and Brecht.[21] His allegiance to a more traditional model is also shown by his constant use of the lexis of the theatre to describe what he is involved in: "theatrical action", "good theatre", "poor production", "the show", "watchable", "well constructed", "dress rehearsal", "characters", and the idea of "staging" (Boal 1998: 224–247). It is also apparent when he describes the efficacious workings of his theatre, where, for instance, there is an "intention to transform the spectator into the protagonist of the theatrical action and, by this transformation, to try and change society rather than contenting ourselves with interpreting it" (Boal 1998: 224). In turn, within the course of the action of the theatre, "the spect-actor is, or must do his utmost to become, the protagonist of the dramatic action" (Boal 1998: 226), which would then "lend itself to an exercise of real action, which is the objective of all forms of the Theatre of the Oppressed" with the ultimate purpose of making "breaches, to open up paths of liberation" (Boal 1998: 225).

The participants in Boal's theatre, therefore, deal with the "here and now" of their own lives, while at the same time they are removed from the actual situation through a definite engagement with theatre. Such involvement, apart from a few examples, was rejected by happeners. One reason for this was because it

20 This would seem to substantiate Heddon and Milling's comment given towards the beginning of this chapter that such participation was a "sign of the times". All three "activities" enjoyed their most active periods in the 1960s and 1970s.

21 In the first three parts of his book Boal details Aristotle's coercive system of tragedy, put to work for the noble ruling class, then moves on to Machiavelli's poetics of virtu, sequestered by the middle classes, followed by a consideration of the subject-object duality of Hegel through to Brecht. In the final two parts, Boal proposes a poetics of the oppressed, where he aims at a more egalitarian, subject-subject relationship.

brought with it a number of habits that were an obstacle to what they were trying to achieve. Kaprow (Kirby 1966: 48), for example, talks about his preference for non-professional actors in his happenings because "They did not have to worry about their 'projectability', (sic) their verbal ability, their 'onstageness', (sic) and so forth". The other reason for its rejection was more pragmatic; the setting up of happening, always with little time to rehearse and never on a big budget, meant that happeners usually had to rely on colleagues and friends as participants, people willing, simply, to get involved in the project.[22]

To sum up, whereas Boal stays grounded in the theatre working to effect change, Grotowski's paratheatre has a starting point in the theatre but at various points goes beyond it. And, it is this less theatrical form of Grotowski's theatre that appears to come closest to the interests of the happeners, especially the more socially and politically orientated practices of Lebel and Vostell.

2.2. The structure of happening, play and a family resemblance

2.2.1. The structure of happening

As was seen earlier, Kirby (section 2.1) states that happening *is* theatre; however, after doing this, he then proceeds to outline how it is different from theatre. One of these differences includes theatre's use of an information structure that is mostly logical, so that it follows a **triangular model** rather than a more open one. A basic structure for the triangular model (Schechner 1988: 25–26), meanwhile, contains at least some of the following qualities: life careers, stories, plot, characters, linear time, action, connections, resolution, dialectic, flow, acting the events, changes through time and causality. The element of conflict, although not given in this list, is also a quality that is important to the "triangular" play (Schechner 1988: 16–17).

Happening, in contrast to theatre and the triangular play, uses a **compartmentalized, alogical information structure** (Pawłowski 1982: 13; 20–21), in which case, there does not have to be a story or any other kind of framework that would help the audience-participants interpret or understand what is taking place. Indeed, it is a disruption which, for Jerzy Limon (2006: 131), makes

22 Kaprow writes about this in terms of expediency first of all, and then as a matter of choice (Kirby 1966: 48–49); Oldenburg follows the same pattern as Kaprow (Ayres 2012); For Kantor and Vostell, it is a matter of choice. See Suchan's (2000: 98) account of Kantor's work with the holidaymakers on the beach at Osieki in the *Panoramic Sea Happening*. Refer to Kaprow's (2003: 163–164) account of how Vostell gathered together participants for his happening, *Berlin Fever*.

happening "a show", as well as a provocation to the theatre and theatricality.[23] Another difference between happening and theatre is the fact that the majority of the roles in traditional theatre are matrixed; that is they owe their existence to the context given by the play, or by the fact that a character is assumed. Happening, for the most part, works outside of this, being more in line with the "great variety of **nonmatrixed** [my emphasis – MB] performances taking place outside of theatre [...] [which function] without creating and projecting an artificial context of personality" (Kirby 1966: 16). Finally, as the information structure in happening is compartmentalized and nonmatrixed, the tension and conflict of theatre does not have a place in happening, or, if there is some form of tension or conflict, it is confined to an isolated event or series of events that do not necessarily elucidate the happening as a whole.

Overall, taking into account the diverse possibilities which have been outlined above, it is possible for happening to occupy an operational space anywhere between efficacy and entertainment and exploit different forms:

- visual art,
- theatre,
- everyday activities from life.

In addition to this, unlike the triangular model more usual for theatre, it can be:

- compartmentalized, with an alogical information structure,
- nonmatrixed.

2.2.2. Happening and play

It can be seen from this attempt to define happening that while it may have its beginnings in the visual arts, it is, in fact, a form that can utilize many different disciplines, both arts based and non-arts based, theatre and somewhere at the edges of theatre, where it actually intersects with "real life" itself. In this "dance" between art forms and the substance of real life, there is a non-partisan playfulness that would also appear to place the **happener** as an excellent example of Johan Huizinga's (1970: 22) *Homo Ludens*, **someone who plays and knows they are playing**, and through this "breaks down the absolute determinism of the cosmos [...][and] confirms the supra-logical nature of the human situation".

23 The third chapter in Limon's book, *Piąty wymiar teatru*, concerns the performance arts and carries the title, *O prowokacji w teatrze i sztuce* (*On provocation in the theatre and art*).

The view that happening is (should be) anything but visual art is also supported by Huizinga's observations about the visual arts. Taking an historical cultural viewpoint, Huizinga (1970: 191) writes that the work of the plastic artist, once finished, is "dumb and immobile" with an "absence of any public *action*" to bring it to life, and where the play element does not exist in either its making or its contemplation. This is because the visual arts are "bound to matter and to the limitations of form inherent in it, [...][which is] enough to forbid them absolutely free play and deny them that flight into the ethereal spaces open to music and poetry" (Huizinga 1970: 190). There are of course voices that would dispute these observations, and Barbara Bolt (2004), who writes about the performative power invested in painting, is perhaps one of these. Notwithstanding this more up-to-date view and the fact that even Huizinga's closest supporters were able to point up some of the more erroneous of his ideas,[24] what Huizinga says in negation of the visual arts, as well as in reference to other art forms, is useful in drawing together some of the ideas about happening given above.

In relation to the visual arts, for example, Huizinga (1970: 191) writes that while "the processes of plastic art run completely outside the sphere of play, [...] its exhibition is necessarily part of some rite or other, a festival, entertainment, or social event", all of which Huizinga invests with playfulness, and which, as we have seen above, Kaprow and Dziamski define as possible territories for happening itself. It would not seem to be without meaning either that what Huizinga writes about the other arts, especially music and poetry, would appear to be more appropriate in relation to happening than what he has to say about the visual arts.

In general terms, Huizinga juxtaposes the "flightless" visual arts with music and poetry which, in relation to play, can *soar* into "ethereal spaces". Indeed, what Huizinga writes about music and poetry could be transferrable to happening in relation to its call for participation and the possibility for fulfilling a function beyond the purely aesthetic. For Huizinga (1970: 191), "The 'music' arts live and thrive in an atmosphere of common rejoicing", with "The emotional effect or operation of their art [...] [being] dependent on a special kind of performance by others or by the artists themselves". He also advises that one should "discard

24 In the introduction to the 1970 edition of *Homo Ludens*, George Steiner weighs up the pros and cons of Huizinga's analysis. In criticism, Steiner comments that in its elitist preferences linked to bourgeois culture, as well as its failure to take on contemporary developments in psychology and game theory, *Homo Ludens* is "in the best and worse sense, a *jeu d'esprit*, the anecdotal discourse of an erudite, somewhat crotchety amateur". In its favour, however, Steiner praises the deep humanity and learning that it shows, which he believes is very much needed in the contemporary world (Huizinga 1970: 13–16).

the idea that poetry has only an aesthetic function or can only be explained in terms of aesthetics", as it fulfils a range of functions, including "ritual, entertainment, artistry, riddle-making, doctrine, persuasion, sorcery, soothsaying, prophecy and competition" (Huizinga 1970: 142). In addition to this, and most importantly for my purposes, Huizinga (1970: 143) sees poets as fulfilling an essential social function "as the educators and monitors of their people".

In spite of the fact that Huizinga refers to functions and roles for music and poetry applicable to antique society, they could also have a more contemporary application[25] relevant to happening. This would then place happening as a performative practice, and one that can also fulfil a transformative function. It also highlights an educational possibility that a number of happeners, but especially Kaprow, advocated (see Chapter 1, section 1.5).[26]

2.2.3. A family resemblance

To conclude this stage of trying to define happening, there is another way of looking at it that ties these disparate possibilities together. Pawłowski (1982: 132, translation – MB) has stated that the "way in which it [the name happening] is used by those who realize happenings as well as its theorists, clearly indicates it is a sign which shares characteristics with those terms that have a family resemblance". This in turn is a concept which appears in Ludwig Wittgenstein's *Philosophical Investigations* when he ponders how the many different types of games, with all of their variations, can still be considered under the one term of "game". Wittgenstein (2009: 36) concludes in the following way:

---

25 The British poet David Constantine (2011) certainly sees a role for poetry that is both monitoring and educational in contemporary Britain. Because of its nature, he sees poetry as being a watchdog to the state, while in schools it is a means of developing critical awareness in pupils. More generally, and not necessarily tied to schools, he sees poetry as teaching us how to "be more fully human".

26 Of interest here is that Kaprow (Kelly 2003: 110–126) considers education in light of Huizinga's ideas concerning play. In addition to this, he makes the distinction between play and game in relation to the education system; contrasting the early years of learning at school, which are fun and play orientated, to the later years and on through the system, which he describes as a competitive game. It is, moreover, a game for power, in which everyone involved in the education system partakes. Kaprow also sees this game orientated mentality as perpetuating a short-term and false worldview, whereas a play orientation, with its focus on selfless participation for its own sake, is one which offers a chance for real change within society. Needless to say, the *artist* as *player*, involved in happening-type activities, has the possibility to be at the forefront of this change.

> And we can go through the many, many other groups of games in the same way, can see how similarities crop up and disappear.
>
> And the upshot of these considerations is: we see a complicated network of similarities overlapping and criss-crossing: similarities in the large and the small.
>
> I can think of no better expression to characterize these similarities than "family resemblances" between members of a family – build, feature, colour of eyes, gait, temperament, and so on and so forth – overlap and criss-cross in the same way. – And I shall say: "games" form a family.

And it is perhaps this application of Wittgenstein's concept to happening that is useful in the search for a definition of happening, as it allows for broad differences to occur between various enactments (happenings/not happenings) and over time, but also allows us to view these enactments as being linked in some way, so that they can be dealt with on an individual basis as well as more generally.

2.3. A set of characteristics for happening and aesthetic-critical possibilities

2.3.1. Characteristics

Adopting a line of thinking that tries to be inclusive of the possibilities for happening, a number of its shared characteristics will now be given. In doing so, ideas put forward by Pawłowski (182: 22–55), Kirby (1966: 11–21) and Morawski (1971b: 124–131) will be presented. These will then be reviewed in relation to the contemporary, postmodern situation as described in Chapter 1 (section 1.1). The provision of such a synthesis is not to ignore or deny the complexities and contradictions pertaining to happening as mentioned in the previous section, rather, it is to provide characteristics as well as draw out ways of interpreting them that will prove useful when thinking about happening in relation to education. To achieve this end, modality will be used to signal possibilities outside of the frameworks suggested here.

In general, happening might be seen to have a number of characteristics:

- *involvement of the public* – the audience are no longer regarded as passive viewers of a performance but *can* take on a more active role, either in their engagement as spectators or actually taking part, becoming, along with the artist, participants;
- *no playing of roles* – unlike traditional theatre, roles in happening *can be* non-matrixed;

- *compartmentalization* – in which the various actions within happening, taking place either together or in separate locations, *do not have to be* linked in any way, or comment upon one another, to form one single narrative structure;
- *abolition of borders between art forms, place and time* – the borders that exist between art forms are dissolved with no one art form taking precedence, so that movement, text, sound, music and painting, *may* all appear alongside one another. In addition to this, happening *may* take place almost anywhere and for any length of time – a few minutes, a number of hours, or even days;
- *element of chance* – allowing chance to be one of the determining factors in organizing and carrying out the happening;
- *objective character of happenings* – the individual elements that make up the happening *can be* treated as objects: movement, behaviour, decorations, light, sound, smell, space and time, can all be objectified, including the people, the participants themselves.

Charles R. Garoian, meanwhile, places such characteristics within the aesthetic sphere and also as part of a modernist enterprise. Concentrating on the interdisciplinary nature of this "performance art" (happening), he writes that

> Although interdisciplinary in its character, modernist performance art confined its critique to the aesthetic assumptions of western European culture. Interdisciplinarity in this instance assumed staying within the parameters of western European epistemology. Its mission to deconstruct the canon and to emerge an aesthetic relevant to twentieth century life resulted in performance art works whose revolutionary concepts contributed to the evolution of the cultural mainstream. (Garoian 1999: 41)

This provides one possible way of looking at happening in terms of a wider cultural perspective and may provide us with a useful point of reference in relation to its operation within an educational setting. However, it is possible to take this same "evidence" and view happening differently.

Referring once again to the characteristics of happening outlined above, the choice of a variety of expressive forms rather than one particular medium as well as the erasure of the line between artist and audience, means that happening can also be placed as a postmodern practice, one that shies away from modernism's grand narrative of high art and, after Jean-François Lyotard (Harrison and Wood 1994: 1000), "the expert's homology", choosing rather diversity and "the inventor's paralogy". Moreover, happening's origins in the late 1950s, amidst the modernist project, does not contradict this. Following Charles Harrison and Paul Wood's (1994: 1000, 1008) argumentation, evolution in the cultural mainstream can be emphasized so that it is possible to place happening within the paradigm proposed by Lyotard where postmodernism is "a form of critically revivified

Modernism, retaining the intellectual prospect of a new form of social existence" (Harrison and Wood 1994: 998–999), one that distrusts metanarratives and wants to "wage war on totality" (p. 990). This would place happening in the postmodern setting outlined in Chapter 1, one in which it is "in the thick of the action", where there is instability in the constant assigning and re-assigning of meaning (objectification and the abolition of borders), an awareness of the fragmented nature of existence (not playing a role or playing a role and compartmentalization), and uncertainty (the element of chance). Indeed, the characteristics for happening given above can also be looked at in relation to (and be seen to equate to) a number of characteristics that Schechner (1982: 120–124) identifies as important to the postmodern and which Garoian (1999: 47–48) transposes into pedagogy. In each case, the Schechner-Garoian characteristics are given in italics:

- the contradictory and complex nature of happening – *paradox*;
- active involvement of the public and actors together – *participation*;
- equality between public and actors, and in the use of different art forms and places (not favouring one above the other) – *indeterminacy*;
- positioning of public and actors as participants allowing for different viewpoints – *multicentrism*;
- the use of different art forms – *interdisciplinarity*;
- compartmentalization and the way that different actions do not have to be linked, the element of chance – *dream logic*;
- emphasis upon active participation rather than passive reception, its nonmatrixed nature, keeping away from one narrative structure and allowing for chance – *process*.

Schechner also gives other characteristics which are not so apparent in happening, and which all relate to a level of self-consciousness. These characteristics are:

- being aware of the processes one is involved in – *reflexivity*;
- using the body as a way of knowing the world (as opposed to simply the mind) – *body intelligence*;
- being aware of the different cultural sites within which one is working or in contact with – *interculturality*.

However, their lack in happening should not necessarily deny its claim to postmodernity as more productive views are provided by Szkudlarek and Rebecca Schneider. Szkudlarek (2009: 12) urges us to view the postmodern not in opposition to the modern, *antimodernist*, but rather something beyond the modern, which opens up new possibilities that were somehow not available to us from the modernist perspective. Additionally, Schneider (1997: 128) writes: "Postmodernism is not beyond the modern but rather 'openly' modern, like a secret explicated".

2.3.2. Aesthetic-critical possibilities

From these perspectives, rather than seeing happening as being either modern or postmodern, it now becomes possible to view it as part and parcel of the same project which, returning to Garoian's idea given above, can either have an aesthetic emphasis or, in accordance with Schneider's pronouncement, be more knowing, more critical in its awareness. And here, Kantor's *Panoramic Sea Happening* which, according to Suchan, questions the nature of happening as it questions the nature of art, or the more politically and socially orientated happenings of Vostell or Lebel, for instance, might be given as examples.[27] Overall then, it is probably useful to think of the possibilities for happening as being at different locations on a grid, where happening, to varying degrees, can be either aesthetic, aesthetic-critical, critical-aesthetic or critical (Figure 1). And, following Wittgenstein's concept, it can also take on any number of the different forms and characteristics outlined above, including those more self-conscious characteristics proposed by Schechner and Garoian. Indeed, Morawski (1971a: 118–120) sees these possibilities as being open to the creators of happenings whether they come from more aesthetically orientated traditions or they are more socially committed and political.

27 Morawski (1971a: 119) sees the Polish (Kantor's) engagement with happening as being restricted to attacks on conventions of culture, while in relation to everyday life or politics they are ambivalent or feign ambivalence.

Figure 1: An aesthetic-critical grid for happening

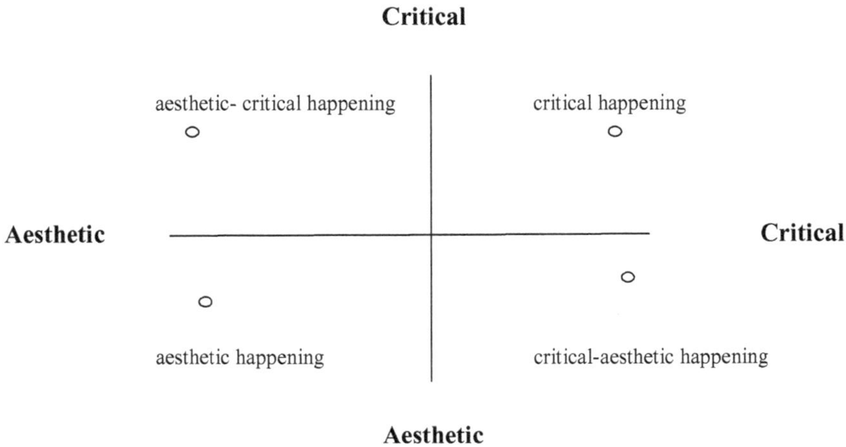

The placement on such a grid, however, is not a stable, once-and-for-all matter, with intentions and meanings being interpreted and reinterpreted both at the time the happenings take place and later, in retrospect. And this is perhaps best illustrated by looking at a number of different happenings, and from various points in time (as well as place), from the late nineteen fifties up to the present.

2.3.2.1. 18 Happenings in 6 Parts

Created by Kaprow in 1959, *18 Happenings in 6 Parts*, can be placed in the aesthetic area of the grid. Indeed, Kaprow's statement about the piece, that it would have no meaning apart from what the audience-participants took from it (see section 2.1.1.1 above), would seem to confirm this. The description of the enactment given by Roselee Goldberg, where the actions themselves are concentrated upon without an attempt at interpretation, also support Kaprow's claim.

In short, the visitors to the subdivided loft space of the Reuben Gallery took their seats. They were designated as part of the cast of a series of 18 happenings that were about to start. A number of figures marched stiffly in single file between the different rooms then took up their individual positions. In one room a woman stood still for ten seconds with her left arm raised, forearm pointing to the floor. Slides were shown in another room. Following on from this, two performers read fragmented and unrelated utterances from hand-held placards. Various musical instruments were played, painters painted on raw canvas set into the walls and gramophones were rolled in on trolleys. After ninety minutes of these simultaneous happenings, four nine-foot scrolls toppled off a horizontal bar between the male and female performers reciting monosyllabic words. A bell rang twice to signal the end of the performance (adapted from Goldberg 1990: 128–130).

However, when Robert Morgan writes generally about American happenings from the fifties and sixties, a more critical note is struck, and in this he highlights Garoian's (1999: 41) idea that the criticism was very much aimed at reinvigorating the existing aesthetic:

> I sense the elation and agitated delight of these events – the expectation that something was in the air, and that the air was in the process of transgressing the normative role of the gallery as a static domicile to merely view works of art. These works functioned as a metamorphosis moving through time. The static relationship of the viewer to the work of art was disappearing, and the participant was being born on the premises of the gallery. These pregnant moments were constantly on the verge of redefining art and always on the cusp of another previously unfelt transition. (Morgan 2012)

There is a real sense, therefore, that the intention was to break the stranglehold of what was classified as art by making the happening include many different references, as well as forms, that would challenge existing art world norms.

*2.3.2.2. Linia podziału (*The Dividing Line*)*

There is a similar sense of challenge to an existing aesthetic in Kantor's *The Dividing Line* (1966).[28] During the happening, as with Kaprow's *18 Happenings in 6 Parts*, a number of actions took place simultaneously.[29] Here however, the challenge was interpreted as not only relating to the aesthetic plane, but as containing a political message. Thus, what was seen by the authors of the happening as something "autonomous, self-contained, neutral" (Baranowa and Stano 2006: 116, translation – MB) was interpreted differently by the then governing, communist authorities. The fact that Kantor had imported an art form from the capitalist USA into Poland in the first place, was seen to be questionable, however,

---

28 The dividing line of the title is informative, being the line Kantor created to segregate that which he himself felt to be good and worthy from that which was pretentious in terms of art. On one side of a blackboard he wrote the names of artists and institutions which were "non-official, not treated seriously, impossible", and on the other the names of those he termed as "pseudoavantgarde" (Pleśniarowicz 1997: 168). Marek Rostworowski builds a grander role and more comic aspect for Kantor, seeing the artist in this instance as sitting as "the final judgement" on the artists and institutions (Baranowa and Stano 2006: 114).

29 For a description of what occurred see Baranowa and Stano (2006: 115).

there were also many references within the happening itself which were seen as attacks upon the communist regime in Poland, and hence political in nature. As Anna Baranowa and Bernadeta Stano (2006: 116, translation – MB) write, commenting on the different events within the happening:

> It turned out that…the covering of the girl lying on the sofa with coal was a symbol of Poland defiled by mining…that the Janiccy brothers eating macaroni from a suitcase were a symbol of the lack of availability of anything else to eat in the shops; while, similarly, the wrapping of Marysia in toilet paper was also a visualization of its lack in the shops […] [however] the greatest outrage was caused by the bricking up of the doorway by Marek and the statement by Igor that the window is barred. – This, of course, demonstrated the situation in socialist Poland.

Whether or not Kantor and his associates were totally free from political intentions in their happening is open to debate. However, this particular example does give an idea of how a happening that is intended to be aesthetic can be seen to contain a critical content. It is also worth noting what Joanna Mytkowska (2000: 60, translation – MB) writes about *The Dividing Line*: "Kantor joined individual events with an anti-institutional and anarchistic speech given during the action. Bricking up the door to the room of the action enhanced the effect of tension and suspense". This does seem to suggest, therefore, that Kantor himself was aware of an effect, over and above the aesthetic, that this particular happening might have.

Whatever the case may be in this particular instance, it does appear that critical and political references can be found, even if they are not advertised or overtly sought by the protagonists. This, in turn, brings up a further element to consider when looking at happenings with a view to their definition-interpretation, and that is the greater context in which they are created. This is certainly true of the happenings by Vostell, as well as by Orange Alternative.

2.3.2.3. Berlin Fever

For *Berlin Fever* (1976), Vostell invited participants from across West Berlin to drive to a field close to the Berlin Wall where they then carried out a number of seemingly unrelated actions. These included the following: slowly driving their cars in tight formation; stopping their cars; removing and then returning a white plate to the boot of their cars; placing a white cloth in front of their cars; putting their plates and a handful of salt on the cloth; driving over the cloth, plates and salt; licking the hand in which they had held the salt while driving; stopping their cars; collecting up the broken plate, salt and cloth; sewing up the plate and salt in the cloth. While doing all of this, meanwhile, the participants were asked to keep a mental note of their actions or write them down. Additionally, and some time later, any notebooks kept during the happening were to be taped inside the boot of the car, with the instruction that the next time the person had a fever they would take it out and destroy it. As part of the happening, the participants were also invited to meet Vostell three days after the event and to bring with them notes of any dreams they had dreamt during that time (adapted from Kaprow, Kelly 2003: 163–164).

Looking at this description, it is perhaps difficult to define the actions as overtly critical or political in any way. In his interpretation, however, Kaprow points to political, social and historical connections, which are built upon his knowledge of Vostell's work and the context within which the happening took place. Indeed, Kaprow (Kelly 2003: 164–165) writes of the "pervasive political references" of this particular piece, which he outlines in the following ways:

> West Berlin's ideological and economic isolation in Communist East Germany; its reduction to an artificial island confined by a wall and three foreign military encampments; the piped-in, superficial affluence in the midst of surrounding austerity and a disadvantaged Turkish working force; an island whose population is dwindling and whose industry is leaving; an island whose artistic culture is imported or pumped up by political machinery, mainly in Bonn and Washington; the island's "fevered" self-consciousness; and saddest of all, its present garrison-town identity compared with the impressive city it once was.

This is definitely a case, therefore, of the wider context in which the happening took place being responsible, in part, for the meanings it contains.

2.3.2.4. Children's Day happening

At first glance, the Orange Alternative gathering on June 1, 1987, in the centre of Wrocław also looks to have nothing to do with criticism or politics. It is simply a gathering of people to celebrate a popular event in the Polish calendar, Children's Day. As such, high school pupils and university students descended on a particular street in the city (Świnicka Street), where they placed red caps upon their heads and started to dance and sing, and give out sweets. They then moved through the crowds singing songs. However, the fact that these actions actually took place and that people felt able to come together to carry them out gave them a significance over and above that of celebrating Children's Day. This has been described by Padraic Kenney (2002: 160), as "a kind of surreal immunity from repression though foolishness", as something "ambiguously political" (Kenney 2011: 104). Indeed, a form of activity that is invested with a particular type of force:

> Anyone who stood in the crowd of an Orange Alternative happening knew at once that this was a transformative, revolutionary experience. It felt, then, as if something new and permanent had been summoned into being, and that the world could never be the same. Chanting "Where are the police?" (as in a happening in June 1988), the crowd performed magic, robbing the police of their power and ascending into a sphere above politics. (Kenney 2011: 102)

There are a number of ideas hinted at in these particular references. First of all, there is a sense of carnival in accordance with Bakhtin, where fun, and especially laughter, have the power to debunk authority.[30] Then, there is the sense that this is something political and not political: as mentioned above (section 2.3.2), something similar to an aesthetic action that also holds a political dimension, or within which one can be discerned. This politically ambiguous dimension might also be an allusion to grassroots interest in seemingly everyday concerns that are aired in a public forum, non-political in the "big sense" of politics, but nonetheless a powerful force. A force which Kenney cites as being as important as other factors in helping to topple the repressive regimes of Eastern Europe,[31] and one which Elżbieta Matynia discusses in her descriptions of the activities of Solidarity in the summer of 1980 in relation to performative democracy (see Chapter 3, section 3.1.1).[32] Finally, in an echo of a happening Kantor witnessed in the early

---

30 Bakhtin (1985: 90) states that laughter in the Middle Ages was a way to combat fear of all kinds including that of authoritarian power, which uses coercion and violence to maintain its position. He also comments that by the time of the Renaissance, this elemental force of laughter, stemming from the people for the people, becomes more self-aware, taking on a critical historical consciousness (Bakhtin 1985: 73).

31 Kenney (2002: 4–5) comments how grassroots social movements changed the rules of engagement with their communist rulers, freeing themselves from the usual sites of opposition and bringing a less serious tone to the whole proceedings. He also writes about concrete examples of opposition in the form of social campaigns in Poland: one against alcohol abuse, another about homelessness, and a third, concerning people on pensions and benefits (Kenney 2002: 48–56).

32 For Matynia (2009: 5), the power of performative democracy stems from the fact that it is ordinary people talking out in public about matters that mean something to them – "local issues" as she calls them. In terms of Poland, by the end of the 1980s, this was "a new space, outside of the homes, churches, and hidden sheds where news and poetry had hitherto been printed. This new space, located between that tight little *private* realm utilized by the civil society of the late 1970s and the *official* realm controlled by the state, was about to be carved out of the large dominions of the state and become lawfully inhabited. In this space it would be safe to discuss what Habermas calls 'critical matters of general interest', and from this space citizens could keep a watchful eye on the authorities" (Matynia 2009: 39).

1970s, there is the idea that contact with this particular Orange Alternative event had the power to change the people and the situation in which they found themselves. And, indeed, what Kantor (2005: 450, translation – MB) wrote of a happening he witnessed in 1972 would appear to hold true for this one also:

> I realized something strange: All those actions, which in life can be justified, have their reason for being, garner social praise, a number of them being prestigious, even 'TABOO' – lose all of this as soon as they are placed beside disinterested action, that is artistic action [happening]!

With all of the happenings mentioned above, placement on the aesthetic-critical grid does depend on one's interpretation and so the perspective one brings to it; it also relies upon **the contexts in which they are enacted**. With the happening by Kaprow, this context is the gallery space itself, as a place in which the happening can be sanctioned as art but also, at one and the same time, where it can act as a question mark as to what art actually is. For the happenings by Kantor, the Orange Alternative and Vostell, the context of living and performing in a totalitarian state, or responding to the situation of being "an island" in such a state (in the case of Vostell), sets the pieces within a highly politicized arena. Therefore, the artistic action, relating to Kenney's judgment, and in accordance with Kantor's reckoning, has a transformative possibility beyond simply the aesthetic. In these particular happenings, but also I would argue, the other happenings mentioned within this chapter, one of the mechanisms at work (play) is something which Vivian Patraka (1999: 109–131) outlines in connection with institution[33] and which owes its conception to Michel de Certeau: a differentiation between the concepts of **place** and **space**.

2.4. The place and space of happening and the limen

2.4.1. The place and space of happening

As far as de Certeau (1988: 117–118) is concerned, place is something fixed where rules are determined (and here de Certeau refers to Pierre Bourdieu's concept of field[34]) and consequently, exclusive of other possibilities. It is, therefore, something

33 In particular, museums linked to the holocaust.

34 David Swartz (1997: 117) sees fields as being structured areas whose organizing principles arise from the various types of capital that come together to produce them. And here it is important to note three points specific to Bourdieu's way of thinking. The first is that these areas go beyond individual institutions, so that they are not limited to a particular building or organization but can include more loosely based social

that does not easily allow behaviours and interpretations beyond those which have already been conceived of or taken into account by the place itself. Space, on the other hand, refers to a much more open dynamic, where multiple options, and perhaps ones not necessarily foreseen, are possible:

> Space occurs as the effect produced by the operations that orientate it, situate it, temporalize it, and make it function in a polyvalent unity of conflictual programs or contractual proximities. On this view, in relation to place, space is like the word when it is spoken, that is, when it is caught in the ambiguity of an actualization, transformed into a term dependent upon many different conventions, situated as the act of a present (or of a time), and modified by the transformations caused by successive contexts. In contradistinction to the place, it has thus none of the univocity or stability of a "proper". (de Certeau 1988: 117)

Importantly too, as Konrad Miciukiewicz (2006: 212) emphasizes, the signification given to "materially structured spaces" is determined by a process of constant negotiation between those people that had them designed and built, and their users, who assign them social meaning.

In essence, the enactment of a happening brings space to place, disrupting the fixed and unequivocal and allowing for the fluid and multivalent. This is something which Garoian (1999: 51), citing Patraka, interprets as putting the subject firmly back into territories which normally transform the subject into object, and which Miciukiewicz (2006: 212) terms "social-subjective spaces". It also gives an idea of the way happening works within the established (establishment) areas of place, exemplified by those happeners working against a mainstream aesthetic, or of happeners performing in a totalitarian state. "Invading" places, be it the gallery, the countryside, the beach or (more likely to be) the street, the enactment of happening opens up a space where, as Garoian (1999: 51) comments, "the politics of inscription and representation can be debated and agency self-determined", while for de Certeau (1988: 42), stories (and here I would place happening as a way of making stories) are constantly organizing "the play of changing relationships

---

groupings. The second concerns capital, which Bourdieu designates as the irreducible forms of power that legitimize a person's actions or position, and which come under four generic types: "economic capital (money and property), cultural capital (cultural goods and services including educational credentials), social capital (acquaintances and networks), and symbolic capital (legitimization)" (Swartz 1997: 74). Field then is the combinations of these different capitals in carrying out a particular activity. And the third point to note is that Bourdieu's concept of field is conflictual in the way that it views social relations, so that people's involvement with one another in any particular field is always going to be competitive (Swartz 1997: 117).

between places and spaces", in a never-ending transformative labour. Certainly, as Kenney perceives it, the happenings of the Orange Alternative can be viewed as a form of sociotherapy, empowering participants, so that ordinary people no-longer feared the communist regime and, through this, were able to find their own routes to opposition. One young mother he quotes would appear to substantiate this:

> [...] I try not to miss any of Orange Alternative's happenings. This is because I want sometimes not to fear the militia and their clubs. I come to convince myself that not every day must be depressing and dirty; I come so that at least once every few months, for a few hours, I can show everyone – and perhaps myself most of all – that I can be just like people somewhere in the ordinary, normal world. I can laugh, have fun, be provocative. I need this for my psychological health. I don't want always to think about the fact that there is no milk for my child. Such a happening, once every few months is an orange alternative to reality. (Kenney 2002: 190)

It is apparent too that this space-place mechanism is not only restricted to engagement with an aesthetic or a totalitarian regime, it also functions, to use the young mother's words, "in the ordinary, normal world". And one can readily surmise here that the world she is referring to is the one of democratically functioning countries where individual freedom is a fundamental belief; the world to which Poland now belongs. In such a world, where the constraints and pressures upon the individual are less well defined or noticeable, there would also appear to be more need to confront and challenge place with space. Indeed, a more recent happening that does this is Teatr Strefa Ciszy's *Postscriptum* (2000–2005) in which a number of male participants of the Strefa Ciszy theatre group were sold to shoppers in various markets in Kraków, Poznań and Warsaw: the idea behind the piece being an exploration of how relationships are formed and maintained in a consumerist society (Tyszka 2006: 26).

2.4.2. The limen and happening

To end this chapter, one more idea will be introduced that is important to understand the space of happening and the involvement of participants, and that is the limen. As we have already seen (section 2.1.1.1 above), Schechner views Grotowski's theatre, in part, to be linked to liminality and the liminoid, where the person involved in paratheatre can be considered to be taking part in a form of traditional rite. Indeed, the limen is a condition more usually connected to ritual and the movement from one particular mode of understanding to another, as a result of which the person who experiences it develops a heightened form of awareness. In connection with this, the anthropologist Victor Turner (McLaren 1993: 300) describes the limen as

> The state and process of mid-transition in a rite of passage. During the liminal period, the characteristics of the *liminars* (the ritual subjects in this phase) are ambiguous, for they pass through a cultural realm that has few or none of the attributes of the past or coming state. Liminars are betwixt and between. [...] Liminars are stripped of status and authority, removed from a social structure maintained and sanctioned by power and force, and leveled to a homogenous social state through discipline and ordeal. [...] Much of what has been bound by social structure is liberated, notably the sense of comradeship and communion, or communitas.

According to Turner, therefore, the limen is a space of ambiguity where time ceases to be important, and within which, for the duration of a particular process, there is a state of equality where hierarchical power structures are placed in abeyance. It is also a space where people feel free from the norms of the community to which they belong. In relating these qualities to happening, they certainly appear to echo some of the characteristics outlined in this chapter, where happenings involve partnership, can occur over almost any timeframe, and where those taking part do not have to take on roles but can be actively engaged as participants – as themselves.

In another passage, Turner (McLaren 1993: 300) describes a concept related to the limen – the liminoid which he attaches to "the many genres found in modern industrial leisure that have features resembling those of liminality [...] for example, theatre, ballet, film, the novel, poetry, music, and art, both popular and classic in every case, and pilgrimage". In addition to this, he states:

> These genres develop most characteristically outside the central economic and political processes, along their margins, on their interfaces, in their tacit dimensions. They are plural, fragmentary [...], experimental, idiosyncratic, quirky, subversive, utopian and characteristically produced and consumed by identifiable individuals, in contrast to liminal phenomena [...], which are often anonymous or divine in origin. (McLaren 1993: 300–301)

The liminoid, then, relates to known practices within industrialized societies that are not mainstream activities but which call into question the mainstream by being done. These practices also allow people to be themselves when they are doing them. Under the umbrella of art, happening might be placed as a subgenre, which can have an aesthetical or critical outlook (see section 2.3.2 above), or both. And, again, as mentioned in connection with the liminal state, participants continue to be themselves in carrying out the happening.

Ideas of participation and transformation which lie at the heart of the limen and liminoid are also of central concern to happening and performance when they are described in relation to education. According to Jeff Kelly (2003: xxiv), for instance, Kaprow views transformative participation as integral to the practice of happening, which, as far as he is concerned, also implies a fundamental educative process. In addition to this, for Kaprow this participation is not a formalized process, but one that "avoids formalist logic, accepts the body as well as the mind, and embraces discipline but relinquishes ego-centered control" (Kelly 2003: xxiv). Meanwhile, Garoian (1999: 40) describes the limen as "a threshold, a border, a neutral zone between ideas, cultures, or territories". It is also a space that is between absolute values, "unstable, indeterminate, and prone to complexity and contradiction" (p. 40). Indeed, in the image of the expanded limen that Garoian (1999: 43) draws in connection with performance practices as sites of intervention, two ideas (idea#1 and idea#2) are juxtaposed across a rectangular space which they enter to create a state of contention. As a result, Garoian (1999: 40) believes, the limen is not for "the anxious" who will use it to assert absolute values, but rather a desirable space for the artist. Referring to the educational aspirations of my research project, I would add that this liminal space is also a desirable space of engagement for educationalists preparing learners for life in a contemporary world which is perceived to be ever-changing and unstable (see Chapter 1, section 1.1).

2.5. Concluding remarks

Happening has a complex nature making it possible to place it as either a form of enactment situated within the visual arts, a type of theatre or anything but arts based, taking its inspiration from "real life". In spite of these diverse possibilities, a number of characteristics for happening can be defined, including active participation of the public, compartmentalization and the abolition of borders between art forms. Additionally, although happening originated when modernism was still in the ascendant, it holds possibilities as part of a postmodern project, where characteristics such as paradox, indeterminacy and multicentrism are prevalent. It also has an aesthetic-critical potential. Moreover, in the way that happening can be "sensitive to" location, it relates to the concepts of *place* and *space* as proposed by de Certeau. Finally, the model of the limen as suggested by Garoian is a way to view the space that is "created" by happening.

In Chapter 3, the idea of happening and the limen will be investigated more fully in terms of the type of participation it might engender. To guide the discussion, elements of Garoian's description of the limen will be used as well as McLaren's concept of the liminal servant.

3. On the threshold – happening into education

In this chapter, the first steps are taken to place happening within an educational setting. In doing so, the characteristics of the limen as proposed by Garoian: threshold, border, indeterminacy and complexity (Chapter 2, section 2.4.2), are used as ways of encompassing and developing considerations concerning the possibilities for happening and education in connection with the socio-political sphere, the individual in relation to others and the objectification that is part of happening. In addition to this, accounts are given of liminality as it is perceived in two educational studies so as to gain a better understanding of how the space – liminality – of happening might function. In developing these ideas, reference is made to the characteristics of happening outlined in Chapter 2.

3.1. Threshold and border

3.1.1. Performative democracy

Comparing the limen to a neutral area that must be crossed, and moreover one that is placed between ideas and cultures, Garoian's description brings to mind one of the images Matynia (2009) cites in her consideration of performative democracy. This is offered in the postscript to her book where she describes Ivo Andrica's bridge over the River Drina; particularly one feature of its structure, the *kapia*, a space at the centre of the bridge where people could sit and talk. She describes this as the "social, cultural and political power" of the bridge: a place of "terraces and 'sofas'" (Matynia 2009: 165), where people of different nationalities, ethnicities and religions who would not normally have a chance to get together could meet. It is

> a place that people did not have to stop at, or come to, but they did. [...] [A] neutral site, in the middle of the bridge, [...] [making] it possible for people to get to feel at home with each other, to look through each other's lenses and to plant the seeds of trust. (Matynia 2009: 166)

Matynia's written description brings us closer to the essence of this space and at the same time, and in part, reiterates what Garoin writes about the limen. Matynia writes of the *kapia* that it

> is a kind of borderland, except that the very notion of a border is here conspicuously absent. Still, a *kapia*, a place on a bridge, is a *threshold*, a turning point, a place of challenge

and transformation. *Kapia* is about horizons, not borders, and in times of crisis it opens up new prospects, new openings to the future. *Kapia* is a lookout, and I do not mean an outpost or a guard, but a place where one can see much farther. (Matynia 2009: 166)

The challenge and transformation that Matynia talks about here are placed in the socio-political arena, relating to the possibilities of performative democracy. Drawing upon the work of Austin (1975), Matynia places the performative first of all in the forum of linguistics, where speech acts are seen not only to carry meaning but also to have an effect. When this idea is linked to democracy, then its ultimate aim is freedom of speech. And when a social dimension is added, for example life under a dictatorship, the performative shows itself when words which are also "a call to action" leave the private sphere and are heard in the public sphere. In this sense it is a continuation of the Habermasian "enlightenment-bourgeois idea (ideal) […], whose main medium was public debate – rational discussion in which equal subjects take part, so that in the event of a confrontation of views they can reach / come to an agreed position, a consensus" (Dziamski 2010: 19, translation – MB). It is also an extension of this, for whereas the Habermasian project is "a particular ideal and also a projection, which allows for criticism of all the participating forms of democracy and to point out the continuing shortfalls / weaknesses of democracy in contemporary society" (Dziamski 2010: 19, translation – MB), Matynia shows us a public sphere being forged in a non-democratic arena. In addition to this, "Deeply rooted in distinct and diverse sociocultural sites, performative democracy is thus neither a theoretical model, a political ideal, nor a tested system of governance, but a locally conditioned process of enacting democracy in politically varied contexts" (Matynia 2009: 8). This is shown most clearly by Matynia in the non-fictional examples of performative democracy she gives: one of her own involvement in the Solidarity movement from 1980 to 1981 and the other of the Round Table Talks that took place in 1988.

Matynia (2009: 2) writes of her experience of living in Poland and being involved in Solidarity as a time of exhilaration for all those involved, where, after years of repression, people began to introduce themselves to each other and talk together in their own way, without, as she puts it, a "powerful facilitator" leading the discussions. As a result, people felt they could now openly speak in public and actually have control of their own speech, ask questions of each other and expect answers, learn from each other and think for themselves. In this way too, Matynia (2009: 3) describes how people started to structure themselves more formally into grassroots political organizations, where argument was the norm and voting took place, in something that "really was self-governance". In addition to this, these newly found freedoms and equality of voice were to become the hallmarks of the Round Table Talks less than a decade later, being an event where there were no privileged seats and where the ultimate outcome was "the dialogue-produced word – [...] a deprivileged consensual word, its lining woven from the thick polyphony of self-suspended words and voices that have conditioned and assimilated each other" (Matynia 2009: 80).

The similarities between the characteristics of Garoian's liminal space and Matynia's performative democracy as exemplified in her descriptions of the *kapia* and the possibilities for action in such a space that can be seen in her descriptions of Solidarity at the beginning of the eighties, and the Round Table Talks, I would suggest, point to the potential for the limen and happening: the act of being able to participate as equals, to communicate and negotiate, compromise and learn from one another, being a conceivable part of its practice. It also points to the inherent political, and for this read democratic nature of such a participation.

3.1.2. Critical pedagogy

In the forms of participation and communication it advocates, as well as the political foundation for her project, Matynia's performative democracy runs parallel to possibilities that can be found in critical pedagogy, especially Henry Giroux's description of it as a project of intervention. For Giroux (2011: 74), pedagogy has moral and political dimensions and is grounded in the wider world, where it has a responsibility to be involved in creating favourable conditions for the existence of agency, both in social terms and for the individual, dealing with problems related to social justice and global democracy. And, while the context for Giroux's project are the iniquities of neoliberalism and the space for exploration offered by pedagogy, rather than life under a dictatorship and grassroots gatherings, there is a similar need for continuous dialogue: "Such a project also suggests recasting the relationship between the pedagogical and political as a project that is indeterminate, open to constant revision, and constantly in dialogue with its own assumptions" (Giroux 2011: 74). In his study *Wiedza i wolność w pedagogice amerykańskiego postmodernizmu*,[35] Szkudlarek also sees possibilities for critical pedagogy, and these are useful to recount here in more detail, as they offer a number of ideas that open up further the space of the limen in relation to happening and education.

Generally, Szkudlarek's (2009: 13) deliberations are bound up in a larger discussion concerning many areas: knowledge, power, freedom; the subject and

35 *Knowledge and freedom in American postmodern pedagogy.*

identity; pedagogy and American postmodern culture, and politics, which he views from a particularly Polish perspective. This, along with the fact that Poland has definitely become a capitalist country since 1989, make his description of such a critical instrument for education at the service of a democratic project extremely relevant to Poland now (Szkudlarek 2009: 33), and apt for a discussion of happening which I view as relevant to and able to fulfil the expressed aims of education in Poland at the present time (see Chapter 1, section 1.3).

Szkudlarek proposes an educational project that goes beyond the adaptive and individualistic preferences of conservative and liberal tendencies in (American) education respectively. Rather, he sees the idea of the deconstructed subject as a means of opening up "a third space" which is "the entry point for an ethical discussion in solidarity [...] as well as the addressee of a form of education orientated towards change, on the transformation of the subject – understood in a political context" (Szkudlarek 2009: 207, translation – MB). Szkudlarek's third space, I would suggest, is also a liminal one and, as such, offers up further possibilities for understanding the enactment of happening in education.

According to Szkudlarek, critical pedagogy sees individuals as living their lives in asymmetrical relations with others, where domination and regulation, either in direct personal contact or through institutions, are the usual forms of association. Moreover, these relations maintain and even reproduce the existing power structures which favour a privileged few. In addition to this, the workings of this mechanism of oppression: through language, behaviour and ownership of material goods, is more often than not hidden from those people bound up in its structures. In such a situation, as Szkudlarek maintains, the emancipatory aspect of education, coupled with the idea of empowerment, figure highly in critical pedagogy as ways of "freeing individuals and groups from social, political and economic oppression" (Szkudlarek 2009: 208, translation – MB). They are able to do this because an emancipatory project based upon poststructuralist theory decentralizes power, placing it in the complex web of everyday social relations and firmly rooting it in the medium of language. Empowerment, meanwhile, creates a situation where both the individual and the group come together in direct contact, where social space is one with the personal. And this, together with the way that it places the subject, Szkudlarek sees as central to critical pedagogy. Returning to a model for happening where multicentrism and a participation of shared involvement are emphasized, then it is possible to see emancipation and empowerment as part and parcel of the subject's engagement in happening. This being the case, it is worth following Szkudlarek's train of thought more closely.

Citing the likes of Stanley Aronowitz and Giroux, Szkudlarek describes a subject which, rather than being the aware and creative individual of modernism, is one caught up in a constant conflict between emancipation and subjugation; where subjectivity is a question of "identity, intentionality and desire [...] [being] deeply political and inextricably linked to the causes of society and culture, which violate the self-conscious space of the so-called humanistic subject" (Szkudlarek 2009: 208, translation – MB). Moreover, from the perspective of postcolonial theory and humanistic ontology, where a subject-object dualism is set up, the empowered subject in critical theory is one which is involved in a particular dialectic; a subject which is, at one and the same time, "open" and "closed". It is open because it is hybrid, dependent and based on process, and closed because of its ontological sovereignty, "I" against "the Other". This dialectic, as Szkudlarek sees it, is itself connected with two distinct forms of freedom in relation to power. The first is based on autonomy, "I" against the freedom of the Other, where the subject is constructed in relation to power. The second, meanwhile, manages to move beyond oppositions of subject-object and individual-society, and – as Szkudlarek writes – affords "freedom from duality together with freedom to change an ascribed identity" (Szkudlarek 2009: 209, translation – MB). This in total, offers up an educational project / process that facilitates as well as supports democracy as a politics of difference: one which encourages individual empowerment, social development and a relation to power that is grounded in the life of the particular society itself; so that it can be both questioned and changed. In this it comes especially close to Matynia's locally conditioned process of enacting democracy, and indeed Szkudlarek places his pedagogical project squarely within this arena.[36]

Suffice to say, Szkudlarek's model brings together both the political and the educational in the facilitation of a democratic project, providing a further

36 In chapter 2 of *Wiedza i wolność w pedagogice amerykańskiego postmodernizmu*, Szkudlarek writes: "If a meaningful pedagogy is to exist in the postmodern world, overall it should deal with a reconstruction of the vision of society, culture, individual and group identities as well as the relations between them" (Szkudlarek 2009: 65, translation – MB). To achieve this, meanwhile, there needs to be a rethinking of the categories employed, e.g. "the general good", "democracy", "citizenship", and what they actually mean. As a result there is a redefining of the idea of the public sphere, taking it away from the limits and exclusions of modernism and restating it in terms of many public spheres; where particular attention is paid to contact between the weaker and stronger parties in such a situation, since "The dynamic of these relations is the key issue to the functioning of democracy" (Szkudlarek 2009: 67, translation – MB).

possibility for the liminal space of happening in education. With his (re)consideration of the subject-object duality, he also signals another line of inquiry that might be successfully pursued in connection with happening in an educational setting, and that is the form of relations that are possible within its liminal space. However, before I move on to that area, Szkudlarek's concern with American pedagogy in relation to Poland, and especially its linking of the individual and society in a democratic project brings to the fore one figure who stands tall both in terms of education but also art, and especially happening, and that is John Dewey.

3.1.2.1. John Dewey – education

Szkudlarek comments upon the link between the ideas of Dewey and critical pedagogy and how this relates to the Polish situation in the following way: "the most important dimension of this thinking **is not** how it can be used to justify the issues of teaching and learning in the Polish tradition but rather the joint pedagogical and political vision of a democratic society" (Szkudlarek 2009: 65, translation – MB). And indeed, according to Zbyszko Melosik (2007: 311–316), it is the concern for the individual within society in Dewey's writings which forms the basis for Dewey's educational-democratic project. Citing Shapiro, Melosik (2007: 316, translation – MB) writes: "the pragmatic philosophy of Dewey can be understood as an attempt at solving the tension between the 'mass integration and individual developmental educational impulses' found in liberal-capitalist societies", democracy for Dewey being less a form of government than a way of living a communal life, "a total way of social life", which also includes respect for the individual. This holistic viewpoint linked to the social, but also inclusive of the individual, lies at the heart of Dewey's projects both for education and art, and, especially in its American version, strongly influences happening.

The holistic in Dewey's thinking about education brings together the form and content of learning, as well as the participation expected, so that the holistic here is much more than merely the sum of its parts. This means that school and society are together, each indivisible from the other. Indeed, this concern shows itself throughout Dewey's writings. In *Democracy and Education*, for example, Dewey (1966: 191) states:

> The scheme of a curriculum must take account of the studies to the needs of the existing community life; it must select with the intention of improving the life we live in common so that the future shall be better than the past. [...] The things which are socially most fundamental, that is, which have to do with the experiences in which the widest groups share, are the essentials.

And further, stressing the reciprocity of the process:

> A curriculum which acknowledges the social responsibilities of education must present situations where problems are relevant to the problems of living together, and where observation and information are calculated to develop social insight and interest. (Dewey 1966: 192)

It also means that learners and teachers work together, with the development of the learner being uppermost. In Dewey's educational model, this translates itself into classes where the outside world is allowed into school, and where active involvement through experimentation becomes the driving force of the learning process rather than a more isolated and passive experience, where, as he writes, "experience is trying – a meaning which is made explicit in the connected term experiment" (Dewey 1966: 139). In *The School and Society*, Dewey (1956: 18) calls for the introduction of "active occupation" into schools, where learning takes place through "directed living", hands-on experience with materials and involvement with other people, instead of "abstract" and "remote" references, which he sees as the usual lot of schools. In addition to this, he stresses the importance of the learner being able to experiment, not only as a means to motivate but also because it gives her/him something that is "more real" in relation to the needs of life outside of school. In a telling chapter from *The School and Society* titled "Waste in Education", Dewey (1956: 75) sums up the situation in the following way:

> From the standpoint of the child, the great waste in the school comes from his inability to utilize the experience he gets outside the school in any complete and free way within the school itself; while, on the other hand, he is unable to apply in daily life what he is learning at school.

In terms of happening, this experimentation might feasibly be translated into its allowance of chance and acceptance of more spontaneous occurrences, which, in its postmodern guise, Schechner sees as an involvement in process. Meanwhile, the opening up of school to the outside world has its equivalent in happening's abolition of borders between art forms (interdisciplinarity), and more strictly, the calls from Kaprow and Vostell that happening should find inspiration from outside of the arts altogether, in everyday life (see Chapter 2, section 2.1). **Happening in school, therefore, might be expected to provide a space for experimentation and where elements of everyday life are part of its enactment**.

Returning to Dewey, allowing experimentation, as well as creating a situation for the interplay between inside and outside school, also has an impact on the learner in that it makes her/him much more active and allows for greater insights rather than if the learner is given abstract facts and figures to learn. In accordance with this, the imagination is also stimulated into action. And this, as

Dewey points out, is not the limited use of the imagination that is thought up and directed by adults, but rather "the medium in which the child lives" (Dewey 1956: 61). In this way, Dewey proposes a mode of *working-learning-being* that not only places the learner at the very centre of the educational endeavour but which is also highly constructivist in outlook: whereby in the learning process learners are involved in creating meaning for themselves and where, furthermore, the role of the teacher is to allow and facilitate situations in which the learner can experience subject matter in a way that means something to her/him and at a level which is appropriate. As a result of which, as Dewey writes in *The Child and the Curriculum*, subject-matter becomes "a related factor in a total and growing experience" (Dewey 1956: 23). These too are possibilities for happening within an educational setting where happening's compartmentalization, with all of its complexity (paradox) acts as a stimulant to the imagination, where instead of being given answers and one-to-one equivalence, its nonmatrixed character and the prevalence of dream logic spur learners on to create their own meanings.

3.1.2.2. John Dewey – art

Placing a consideration of Dewey's thinking about education here is not only the result of his importance for critical pedagogy, nor the fact that for Polish pedagogues he provides a means, through the medium of education, of building a democratic society that is relevant to its citizens.[37] Dewey is also an important figure linking education to art. For Philip Jackson (1998), for example, it is clear that when Dewey writes about people in contact with art, the philosopher is describing educative experience. More than this, contact with art offers us "indirect lessons about fashioning the more mundane aspects of our lives" (Jackson 1998: 6), which it is able to do because for Dewey, according to Jackson, art offers us meaningful experience and broadens our horizons, whilst also providing a record of previous encounters with life which can act as a guide for those who are interested (Jackson 1998: 5–6).

---

37 Melosik hints at the constant (re-)construction that lies at the bottom of the democratic society and education envisaged by Dewey when he writes that for Dewey, "Democratic society and democratic education do not have a pre-given and absolute form; indeed, the opposite is true, their 'participatory' and 'emergent' character gives them an air of inherent and constant change" (Melosik 2007: 316, translation – MB). In essence then, it is up to each generation to remake democracy anew by their active participation, school and the type of education it offers being an integral part of this whole process.

Dewey's thoughts on art contained in *Art as Experience*, as with his concerns in education, also display a strong democratizing strain. For instance, he writes that one of his aims is "to restore continuity between the refined and intensified forms of experience that are works of art and the everyday events, doings and sufferings that are universally recognized to constitute experience" (Dewey 1958: 3). In doing this, meanwhile, he argues that art and aesthetics need to become reconnected to everyday existence if they are to become relevant and real to people once again (Dewey 1958: 9). This is a reconnection to the real world that Jolanta Kruk sees as having an instrumental dimension, where art has a practical application, being "one of the forms through which the human being orders their relations to the world" (Kruk 2008: 138). In addition to this, as in his writings about education, Dewey emphasizes the need for the individual to be involved in the surrounding world if she/he is to fulfil their true potential. An involvement that is also, in Dewey's opinion, at the very foundation of art. He writes:

> Experience in the degree in which it *is* experience is heightened vitality. Instead of signifying being shut up within one's own private feelings and sensations, it signifies active and alert commerce with the world; at its height it signifies complete interpenetration of self and the world of objects and events. (Dewey 1958: 19)

The experience that art shows, therefore, is the essence (idealization) of those qualities found in common experience (Dewey 1958: 11). The interpenetration mentioned above, meanwhile, is something that Kruk (2008: 138) equates to the Heideggerian "being-in-the-world", while art, as well as other activities influencing social awareness, such as education, was, according to the pragmatists, "to lead to the creation of an enduring mechanism supporting social harmony [...] in which the individual is able to accept their individual needs with the demands of society" (Kruk 2008: 141, translation – MB). A view of art that not only attributes a practical function to it, but also one that links it to a vision for democratic change that lies at the heart of pragmatism.

That these particular ideas with their strong leanings towards democracy are ones inherent in happening, especially in its American guise, should perhaps come as no surprise. Kaprow is described by Kelly as struggling to understand the relevance of Dewey's ideas about art in terms of his own practice. As Kelly (2003: xi) states, "Kaprow grounds himself in American pragmatism", the insights into the art he wanted to practice finding their genesis in Dewey's *Art as Experience*, a book which the artist owned and in which he wrote his own thoughts concerning art, "such as 'art not separate from experience...what is an authentic experience?...environment is a process of interaction'" (Kelly 2003: xi). In addition to this, the characteristics of happening – as placed above in relation to the socio-cultural, political and educational interests of Matynia, Szkudlarek and Dewey – also lend themselves to, and would even seem to facilitate, a process that is democratic.

3.2. Indeterminate and complex

As mentioned in the previous section, Szkudlarek's interest in the issue of subject-object duality signals another line of inquiry that might be successfully pursued in connection with happening in an educational setting: the form of relations that are possible within its liminal space. This area, therefore, will now be considered. In doing so, concepts of "the other" and "the outsider" will be touched upon as well as the issue of ethical relations between partners. Because the form of objectification happening promotes is problematic, especially if it is to fulfil a contemporary democratic agenda, this area is also examined.

3.2.1. Contact with "the other"

The possibilities created by being situated on the threshold / border are something that Witkowski (2000) considers in his critical project for education (in Poland) which he outlines in *Uniwersalizm Pogranicza.* Here, in a close consideration of Bakhtin's works concerning Dostoevsky and Rabelais,[38] Witkowski takes the lessons to be learnt from a wider cultural setting and applies them to the educational arena. In doing so, he rejects the idea that a living culture can be placed at the centre to become an isolated entity, insulated from "the other". Instead, as Witkowski would have it, culture must be practised at the borders if it is to maintain its vigour and relevance: "the quality of life in and of culture can be measured against our ability to exist 'at the border', at the 'threshold', facing the boundary which itself poses a real problem to us in its full cultural dimensions – where, how and why it is worthwhile to live and be active" (Witkowski 2000: 202). Meanwhile, this ability to exist at the border opens us up to "the whole cultural complexity of life with a permanent co-presence of existential tensions and 'earthquakes', constitutive for the dynamic of life in its integrity" (Witkowski 2000: 202).

This destabilized and complicated state is reminiscent of the one that Garoian attributes to the limen. And certainly, Witkowski creates a picture of tension and entanglement, as well as self-doubt in relation to the other (and for the other, read the ideas placed at either side of Garoian's limen) when he describes a life

38 *Problems of Dostoevsky's Poetics* (1984) and *Rabelais and His World* (1984).

lived on the border. To relate the full force of Witkowski's (2000: 18, translation – MB) ideas I will quote him at some length:

> I get to know myself through experience in constant amazement or self-confirmation of how far my tolerance of the other stretches – so that the question of a deepening self-knowledge is not just simply: what do I really believe or what is my essential and already shaped centre, but how far and where [...] do my borders lie? Where are the borders of my world? Who do I allow across that border, who do I simply tolerate and who do I not allow across and why? As a result of this also, am I not impoverishing myself? And how am I to know and confirm this? What does my own private customs and border control for strangers look like, and how do I fare when I have to undergo this control myself? What level of safety do I need to maintain, and how afraid should I be when somebody "uncalled for" enters my world [...]? What happens when the other turns out to be alien and even more than this, an enemy? Is my source of fear for the other also his source of fear for me? And is it really only ever between us? Is it our shared guilt? And does it start by the way in which I treat "myself" and my defenceless-ness in relation to myself?

Witkowski's contact with "the other", as well as the dialogue that ensues, is different from Matynia's, however. Whereas Matynia describes a process in which "assimilation" and therefore compromise are part and parcel of discussion, Witkowski offers an alternative where there does not have to be agreement. As Witkowski (2000: 14, translation – MB) writes of this "uncomfortable" form of dialogue: "The partner in real dialogue may be life-enhancing and inspirational, without being transparent and unambiguous, without giving the chance of consensus, while pushing their parasitical culture upon you". As a result, the question we ask of our partner in dialogue, "what does he mean?", always needs to be accompanied by the question to ourselves "what do I mean?", which creates a situation where neither a reduction nor an understanding of the other is reached, but rather where there is "an intensive relation to the other for oneself" (Witkowski 2000: 15, translation – MB). This opens up in turn, **a possibility in the limen of happening for participants to work together, but also maintain their separateness: the compartmentalization of happening and its nonmatrixed character facilitating this form of interaction**. In doing so, it seems to me that the type of dialogue Witkowski describes is also close to the hermeneutic discourse about which Robert Kwaśnica writes.

For Kwaśnica (1995: 23–24), the truth about what something is, its ontology, can only be revealed through discussion; one, moreover, that is based on difference, **hermeneutic discourse**, rather than aiming towards one point of view, **constructive argument**. This is because it is only through hermeneutic conversation, allowing for many different perspectives, that the complexity of things, and therefore their true nature, can hope to be uncovered (Kwaśnica 1995: 13–15). In this case, difference has a vital and various roles:

- difference is a divided understanding of the world, one which makes possible a communal sense of belonging, because understanding is a shared responsibility;
- difference is something positive, as it means each of us is responsible for another possible understanding of the world; so that through language, each of us is a witness for other people (and vice-versa), uncovering possibilities beyond individual borders of understanding;
- involvement in this kind of dialogue means that differences are dealt with not to escape from them, but to uncover understandings of the world that are normally hidden from us, to learn from them truths about ourselves and the community of communication to which we belong;
- in terms of learning we are involved with knowledge different from our own, not to assimilate and improve what we have, but to find out its (the different knowledge's) particular truth; so the question in this case is not to what degree knowledge is true, but rather what truth it contains and why that particular truth and not some other;
- initiating and taking part in such a discussion we are involved in another world, which we enter and then return from; therefore we cannot foresee, let alone plan, how our understanding will be changed (Kwaśnica 1995: 25–26).

Associating Kwaśnica's ideas with happening, its liminal space would be one that embraces difference. The area where ideas meet being a space of shared responsibility for understanding, an extending of understanding rather than its narrowing down, and the revealing of understandings that would normally be hidden. It would also be a space in which to question the ideas (truths) we come into contact with, as well as an involvement with unforeseen (unforeseeable) consequences.

To try and gain a further idea of what relations in difference might entail, as well open out the idea of "the other" from Witkowski, a number of Rutkowiak's ideas concerning "the outsider" will now be considered.

3.2.2. Relations with "the outsider"

For Rutkowiak (1997: 88), relations with the other, whom she terms *outsider*, fall into four categories: the **researcher**, the **ethical partner**, the **reformer**, and the **catalyst**. With the first, the outsider is like a researcher (Rutkowiak 1997: 88–92) getting to know those who are unknown to them. In outlining this particular form of relation, Rutkowiak chooses to ask who actually makes the best researcher: is it a person who is part of a group and knows it intimately, or is it someone who is an outsider who has nothing to do with the group at all? There are, according to Rutkowiak, advantages to both positions. The former will be sensitive to the group's existing qualities and needs, while, on the other hand, it will be easier for the outsider to give a more unbiased picture of the group. The conclusion Rutkowiak reaches is that the best researcher would be a mixture of both the insider and the outsider. Meanwhile, in connection with happening this would appear to open up the possibilities of egalitarian relations between those involved in happening, those who are familiar with the form and those who are unfamiliar with it working together on an equal footing.

As Rutkowiak (1997: 92–94) describes them, relations on the ethical plain allow us to see ourselves more clearly through comparison with the outsider, and come close to Witkowski's concept of the other given above. Drawing upon the philosophy of Emmanuel Levinas, she promotes a subject-subject relation where, as with Witkowski, the people who come together never give themselves up or lose themselves to the other, even though they are intensely involved. Here, Levinas' own words, cited by Rutkowiak, are informative. Writing about Eros as a model for intense relations, Levinas states:

> Love then, does not lead to an object relation, one in which the other person becomes mine, subordinate to me, withdrawing their secrets. Neither does it cut the cords of contact between us, but creates ones of a new quality, with elements of "Not-knowing-the other" and unpredictability. (Cited in Rutkowiak 1997: 92, translation – MB)

In addition to this, for Levinas, the other "'...is not a second me'. He is, rather, free, 'a Foreigner', over whom I have no power, and with whom I do not have a 'shared fatherland'" (Rutkowiak 1997: 92, translation – MB). Vital to this form of contact is language, as it is language which allows relations on this metaphysical level to exist and develop. Taking into account Rutkowiak and ethical contact, and considering the contact to be experienced in happening, it might be expected that participants would feel encouraged to put forward and discuss their own ideas and points of view, whilst also being open to and respecting those of their fellow participants.

Pragmatic relations (Rutkowiak 1997: 94–96) refer to contact with the outsider that changes the other person or that person's surroundings, so that the outsider in this case is a reformer. Referring to the work of Claude Lévi-Strauss and Edward Said, Rutkowiak grounds this particular option for the outsider in ideas stemming from classical anthropology and colonial studies. The former is informed by an interest in other cultures and attempts to describe their lives and social structures objectively. Taking into account this point of view, Rutkowiak states that the other, in this case so-called "primitive societies", were seen as something "wild", "good" or "original", while whatever the judgment about them, there was an urge to try and look after them or civilize them, to make their lives better. In terms of colonial studies, colonization is seen to be the result of western European expansionism and the underlying need for profit. Meanwhile, to justify this whole process, concepts of the colonized were created which were effectively based on the colonizers' ideas rather than what actually existed. In this instance, Rutkowiak's pragmatism, connected to the outsider is a call not to lose sight of the person as subject in our relations with them, especially in connection with what they themselves have already accomplished. In terms of contact between people in happening, pragmatic relations would mean that participants would not impose their views upon each other, either about a particular theme or situation or who the other participants actually are.

The final category that Rutkowiak (1997: 96–98) proposes for the outsider, a catalyst for the self-education of the subject, is one in which one person helps another person find themselves; aiding them to reconstruct their experiences, change their convictions or views, or simply work towards change within themselves. As Rutkowiak points out, from a traditional perspective, the teacher in school is the archetypal outsider, from whom the learner receives information about the achievements of their culture. With this particular idea of the outsider in connection with schooling, however, Rutkowiak (1997: 97) poses the question of whether the teacher is the "accepted (acceptable) outsider", supporting the existing system and helping their pupils adapt to (and adopt) that system, or whether the teacher is a "provocative outsider", creating resistance within pupils that can lead to changes in their understanding and points of view. In addition to this, Rutkowiak also connects sociological conversion to this particular idea of the outsider, where an educator might be someone who "brings about a change in identity and creates a transformation in the individual" (Rutkowiak 1997: 97, translation – MB). Once again, relating this version of the outsider to happening, there is a sense in which this points to an adaptive (adoptive) function for happening or one which is transformative, in which case it is conceivable that the enactment of the happening will either assist in the upholding and perpetuation of an existing (school) system or lead to a greater critical awareness among participants.

Summing up this consideration of Rutkowiak's outsider in relation to happening, it highlights the possibilities for:

- egalitarian relations between participants,
- encouragement for one's own ideas and openness to the ideas of others,

- a space where participants do not impose their views upon one another,
- the selection of either an adaptive (adoptive) or transformative function.

3.2.3. Personalism and semiotics

Interestingly, there are two aspects in Rutkowiak's account of the outsider that are echoed and extended by Witkowski's reflections upon "the other" and dialogue that began this section above, and which, I would suggest, throw further light upon the possibilities within the limen of happening. These include the subject-subject relation between dialoguers in Rutkowiak's ethical category and the transformative possibilities offered by the outsider as catalyst. Witkowski's deliberations, however, move into the arenas of **personalism** and **semiotics**, when he differentiates between the dialogue of Martin Buber and that of Bakhtin. Witkowski (2000: 56, translation – MB) writes:

> real dialogue as understood by Buber could only come into being thanks to the establishment of relations between the *I* and the *You*, that is between a partner and a participant [...] relations between replicas not being the same as they are between persons [...]. In this way, Buber's dialogue was definitely different to many other and similar conceptions of dialogue, among others [...] Mikhail Bakhtin, who in *Problems of Dostoevski's Poetics* also found dialogical relations between fictional literary figures [possible]. With Buber however, the basis for dialogue was the relation between persons.

He continues:

> It seems that this difference allows one to avoid the one-sided personalistic reading of communicative subjectivity in the conception of Bakhtin [...]. For Buber it is fundamental to understand dialogue as the unmediated being in relation, while for Bakhtin it always seems to be the self as a sign mediated through the sphere of "the quoted word". (Witkowski 2000: 56, translation – MB)

This – I would suggest – opens up two further possibilities for reading the forms of engagement within the limen of happening; one where the person is in direct relations with the other, and the second where the person is a sign, caught up in a system of signs. Could the limen of happening create a situation where participants can be, at one and the same time, involved in relations (subjectively) with one another and, knowingly, part of a greater system of meaning? A system, moreover, that according to Bakhtin is not confined to the immediate "text" but transverses beyond it, thereby allowing a more critical, and by extension, transformative edge. This would certainly connect with Szkudlarek's proposal for a critical pedagogy where there is a "knowing" subject, also conceding to happening a form of reflexivity that places it as a contemporary, postmodern practice.

Moving on from Witkowski and concentrating more fully on Buber, his ideas about relations might also go some way to explain the seemingly contradictory possibilities within happening, namely, the subjective and objective relations that appear to be possible at one and the same time. In the practice of happening, when the audience-participants and artist take on more equal roles, I would suggest the *I-Thou* relation of Buber is a possibility. Meanwhile, when the audience-participants are treated as objects by the artist, the *I-It* experience is primary. And, although there is a problem to pin down exact meaning in "a poetical work" (Buber 1937: xii) like *I and Thou,* Buber does seem to suggest that a constant movement in and out of *I-Thou* and *I-It* relations are a particular characteristic of the work of art, which exists both in personal relation to the beholder (and for happening we might write active participant) but also as a separate entity:

> In art the act of the being determines the situation in which the form becomes the work. Through the meeting that which confronts me is fulfilled, and enters the world of things, there to be endlessly active, endlessly to become *It*, but also endlessly to become *Thou* again, inspiring and blessing. It is "embodied"; its body emerges from the flow of the spaceless, timeless present on the shore of existence. (Buber 1937: 14)

Are the participants involved in happening, a living art / non-art (live art), constantly moving between this *I-Thou* relation and *I-It* experience?

3.2.4. Happening and objectification

Since the objectification that takes place within happening is one of its characteristics (see Chapter 2, section 2.3.1) but also one that problematizes both the possibilities of a subject-subject relationship as well as the agency it allows participants, the idea of what this objectification might entail will now be explored. To do this an argument based within the practice of painting and developed by Bolt is employed: this calls for an art that goes beyond representation to one that is performative. Ideas put forward by Kruk concerning the aesthetic and education in relation to Martin Heidegger and Dewey are also presented. Additionally, a more radical perspective offered by Ewa Domańska in which she considers the performative turn in the humanities is included.

Bolt (2004) is primarily concerned with art as a performative practice, and throughout her book, *Art Beyond Representation: The Performative Power of the Image*, she describes the art making process as non-representational. It is non-representational for Bolt, in the sense that in making ("doing") art, the choices made and the actions taken by the artist do not follow a prescribed course of action, nor are they tied to a preconceived outcome, rather they are the result of an intimate interaction between the artist and her tools in the production of the final painting. Describing the creative process in this way, substantiating her ideas by referring to the work of Heidegger, I believe Bolt presents concepts that can be helpful in trying to understand more fully the objectification that takes place in happening.

Using the concepts of "setting-before" and "being-in-the-world", Bolt argues that the artist does not have to be involved in a representation that is about fixity and mastery, where "whatever-*is*" is an object for the person-as-subject (setting-before). Rather, she advances the idea that understandings which arise from handling or the practice of work (being involved in the act of painting and, I would argue, the enactment of a happening) are in a different paradigm to those of a commonly accepted representation, shifting the balance from "representation as a mode of thought to representation as bodies in process" (Bolt 2004: 14). In this, through Heidegger, she also asks us to return to the pre-Socratic Greek world, where humanity was looked upon by what-*is*, rather than what-*is* being the object of humanity's scrutiny, as it is today. This is because "In the company of what-*is*, man is neither privileged nor detached, but rather merely exists among other things" (Bolt 2004: 20). It is this position of "being-in-the-world", **non-privileged and existing among other things**, I would suggest, that offers a way of understanding the form of objectification operating in happening.

It is informative here also to refer once again to Kruk and her considerations concerning the aesthetic and education. Kruk (2008: 137), too, refers to Heidegger and his idea that "setting-before" is an attempt to describe the objectifying relation that can exist between people and things; causing a dualism that separates the inquiring subject from the external world, which, in turn, leads to a technical, instrumental engagement where "Man the exploiter gives nothing of himself, his relation with things being one of ambivalence, because he is only dealing with objects of use" (Kruk 2008: 31, translation – MB). A form of involvement that Kruk sees as the predominant one in today's world. This is in contrast to the involvement that comes with the creation of the work of art, where, echoing Bolt's idea that the practice of the artist is not representation as a mode of thought, she states that "the activity of the artist always comes before thinking and its search for an appropriate form in relation to itself" (Kruk 2008: 31, translation – MB). The result is that whereas

> Both the work of art and the technical work have a material character, [...] they are the effect of two different forms of human reflection. "Pure technique" is not based on discovery, but rather the total uncovering of the ways of the world. The work of art comes into being as the search for something that is rooted beyond the technical sphere. (Kruk 2008: 31, translation – MB)

This offers a further view of what the objectification in happening might entail, where it is **not for exploitation, which is more usual for practices of the contemporary world,**[39] **but an attempt to discover something beyond that world.**

A development of this idea is also offered by Kruk when she explicates Dewey's pragmatism with regard to the aesthetic, which, as we have seen above, also has implications for the democratic/democratizing nature of Dewey's educational project. For Dewey, unlike Heidegger, emphasis on the "usefulness" of materials is not a danger, as "the technical objectifying of things in the pragmatic version becomes an **affirmation of tools** [my emphasis – MB], which are a synthesis of human thought and action" (Kruk 2008: 139, translation – MB). This means that "things created by humans [...] have an instrumental worth, which is shown in their effectiveness in satisfying our needs" (p. 139), something which is as true for everyday objects as it is for the work of art. As Kruk (2008: 138, translation – MB) writes:

> Dewey's thesis concerning the "practicality" and "usefulness" of art is not contradictory. It stems from his understanding of the idea of the practicality of art, which is simply one of the ways for the human being to organize relations with the world. And, because nature and art/culture are not contrary to one another, the experience of art is useful in a universal way, such as *being-in-the-world* is universal.

From this perspective, the objectification occurring in happening is not detrimental to the individual, rather it is **openly and positively instrumental; the objectifying of things and people serving an educational purpose, that of knowing more about the world in which we exist.**

Yet another perspective for the objectification that takes place within happening is offered by Domańska's (2007) consideration of the performative turn in the humanities. Domańska gives three proposals concerning the subject, where traditional distinctions between what is and what can be subject and/or object are blurred, or lost completely, so that there is no distinction between subject-object but rather a bond of mutual cooperation through action.

The first situation Domańska presents is one in which the humanities are moving away from a textual analysis of the world to one in which they are trying to understand it in a direct way, unmediated. What is more, this is a world which is swiftly moving, extremely complex and open to dramatic change. Here the traditional view of the human being alone as subject is lost. Subject status is now

39 For a succinct explanation of this situation see Greaves (2010: 149).

shared and encompasses a whole range of hitherto unimagined and unimaginable "bedfellows": animals, clones, cyborgs, mutants, terrorists, even inanimate objects, in their "own subjectivity" (Domańska 2007: 54). In addition to this, for Domańska, the subject of the performative turn is not a passive, contemplative entity, but one which is dynamic, prone to change and revolution. At the same time, the essential, homogeneous subject of previous incarnations is transformed. This is a new kind of subject, one which is strong and a hybrid, "created in *happenings*, events, [...] not a spectator but an initiator and agent. Neither is this subject a 'lone subject' (the romantic subject), rather it always acts together with other subjects and 'actors' (with human and non-human entities)" (Domańska 2007: 56, translation – MB). It is also important to realize that these non-human-entities-become-subject, have not undergone some form of anthropomorphism or simply been endowed with human intentionality, rather there is a recognition that changes in reality take place as a result of "cooperation between different kinds of subjects with agency" (Domańska 2007: 57, translation – MB). Further to this, and relating to ideas put forward by the American philosopher of science, Andrew Pickering, Domańska (2007: 58, translation – MB) writes about non-human subjects: "All of them are agents acting in different ways, which are not the same as human ways of acting. [...] (human beings act but non-human entities also act)".

Returning to happening, perhaps this gives another perspective on the objectification that takes place. Rather than perceiving it as "a making of objects" of all participants be they human or non-human entities, so that they can be manipulated at will by some "omnipresent puppet master", the equalling out that takes place might be seen as occurring in the opposite direction. The liminal space of the happening, being at one and the same time the space open to the performative turn, **allows all participants (human and non-human) to become active subject-agents, working in cooperation**.

3.3. The limen and the liminal servant

In this outline of the limen and the possibilities for happening given so far, various perspectives have been considered. These have included the socio-cultural, political and ethical. In addition to this, a number of these have had their basis in theorizing related to education. It is now time to step more firmly into the educational arena and examine considerations of the limen that have arisen out of two theoretical-empirical studies of actual schooling practices: one in Canada and the other in Poland. In the former, the concept of the teacher as a liminal-servant is also introduced and discussed.

3.3.1. The limen in school

In *Schooling as a Ritual Performance: Towards a Political Economy of Educational Symbols and Gestures*, Peter McLaren (1993: ix) uses a mixture of "anthropology, alchemy, ritual studies, and post-structuralism" to present an ethnographic study of the students and teachers in a middle school in Toronto, Canada. Pivotal to his research, meanwhile, is the concept of liminality.

As was seen at the end of Chapter 2, the limen is a space where normally accepted forms of being and activity are suspended to be replaced by ones which are less easy to identify. As a result of this, it is unstable, with the usual structures of power becoming dislocated, overtaken by a spirit of community and more equal relations. Additionally, because of its neutrality (after Garoian), it is a space within which different ideas can readily be explored.

In his study of predominantly Portuguese learners, McLaren identifies different states of interaction that take place within the school. These include the streetcorner state, the student state, the sanctity state and the home state.[40] It is in the streetcorner state in opposition to the student state, however, that McLaren (1993: 94) sees the liminal dimension at its most pronounced, offering among other things, the **subjunctive mood**[41] compared with the **indicative mood**; ritual forms which are flexible, haphazard and improvisational as against those which are conventionalized, stereotyped and formal; the tapping of one's own inner resources (right lobe emphasis) as opposed to imitation of teachers (left lobe emphasis), and communitas (repartee) versus anomie and anxiety.

In his description of the streetcorner state, McLaren also brings to life Bourdieu's concept of **habitus**, that is a set of ways of thinking and acting – dispositions – that are conditioned in early socialization (Swartz 1997: 103).[42] These

40 It is important to note that McLaren (1993: 93, 102) does not see these states as autonomous but rather seamlessly interwoven, so that students are constantly moving back and forth between them as they progress through the school day. McLaren's need to delineate the states so strictly, as he comments, is for the purpose of his discussion.

41 I would place McLaren's subjunctive mood as a metaphor for both creativity and lateral thinking. In a fuller explanation of its characteristics he states "it is one that embraces fantasy, experiment, hypothesis, and conjecture. In this mood of 'may-be', metaphors flourish and promote novel cultural forms […]. There is apt to be more 'flow' […] in the matching of skills and abilities since students do things at their own pace. Students spend time experimenting with different roles – playing 'as if' they were others. Yet students are most decidedly themselves in this state" (McLaren 1993: 88).

42 Swartz (1997: 103) quite succinctly defines habitus as a set of "structured structures" that are also "structuring structures".

dispositions are the internalization of external structures that dictate what is possible (and not possible) for a person from a particular strata of society to be involved in and accept, and how that person might behave. McLaren hints at such an idea, although he does not state it, when he writes about the lack of control students actually have in either the streetcorner or student state, as in both the "students are already 'cooked' (i.e. their roles are informed by their social experience in the sense that they sustain a set of social standards expected of them by both their peers and the authorities)" (McLaren 1993: 90–91).

McLaren's portrayal of the streetcorner state also appears to illustrate something which Michelle Lamont and Annette Lareau (1988: 157) refer to as "marginal high status signals" to show their difference to Bourdieu's examples of cultural capital, which is the domain of the more advantaged middle and upper-middle classes rather than the working class.[43] In the streetcorner state especially, McLaren creates a vibrant and frenetic picture of the behaviours, physicality and social encounters that take place, and which are in opposition to the student state that is sanctioned by the field of school. The student state, for example, is more formally organized and rigid in terms of movement and time, creating a space where emotional display is frowned upon and where hard work is promoted. It is also a state within which the outward display of being part of a community plays little role and where, generally, there is a division between mind and body.

By citing Bourdieu's concepts in relation to McLaren and the liminal space he is suggesting for his streetcorner state, I do not, however, want to claim a particular class status for the limen, nor happening for that matter. Rather in this context the limen becomes a site of "conflict", where forms of behaviour, physical activity and community which are seen to be opposed to the field in which they take place (here it would be school-based education), are allowed and utilized, taking on (and here I believe the two meanings of the phrase are valid: "to fight" and "to become") the legitimate culture. This then opens up the way for a liminal space in the enactment

43 Lamont and Lareau (1988: 157) write: "It is important to note in this context that we believe that lower class high status cultural signals (e.g. being streetwise) perform within the lower class the same exclusivist function that the legitimate culture performs in the middle and the upper-middle class. However, for the purpose of clarity, the term cultural capital is not applied to these signals because they cannot be equated with the legitimate culture. A new concept needs to be coined for these signals; 'marginal high status signal' is a potential candidate". I believe this is applicable to the Azorean students because, as McLaren (1993: 88) describes them in the streetcorner state, they appear to possess sets of behaviours, symbols and so on that confer status, e.g. "The cool guys like to fight".

of happening in education that is not simply reproductive of school forms and norms: "it is like that, because it is school" (Klus-Stańska 2012: 36, translation – MB), but allows for more flexible and creative approaches that involve both pupils and teachers working responsively together; a situation that education wants to promote (as outlined in Chapter 1) but finds difficult to, or cannot instigate.[44] These ways of working and the co-operation involved would also facilitate part of the "margin of freedom" that Maria Mendel (2007: 61, translation – MB) states comes with the negotiation of relations within institutions, a space of the "allowable unallowable, possible impossible". An area for a more human contact, which Mendel (2007: 101, translation – MB) sees as coming through ritual, being an antidote to yet another part of "our" world, school, that is supposed to be "institutionalized and rational, and decidedly 'non-magical' ".

This idea of the limen as a site of rupture where people and ideas are brought together in a transformative atmosphere is dealt with by Mariusz Dembiński (2005) when he considers liminality in relation to **ritual in the context of lessons in Polish schools**. Basing his theoretical empirical study on the work of McLaren, Turner and Arnold van Gennap, Dembiński concentrates upon the lesson in terms of sub-ritual, focusing on the different events-interactions that take place in lessons generally, as well as providing a "provisional model" for researching the lesson as a microritual, a contained entity of 45 minutes. In doing so, he also provides a rich terminology which might also be applied to the liminal space of happening.

For Dembiński, the whole of school is involved in a ritualizing process where its participants, irrespective of whether they are teachers or students, move beyond the obligatory structures of society in a process of marginalization, thus becoming different to what they had been before the ritual started. Importantly,

44 McLaren (1993: 85) writes of St Ryan that it was decidedly traditional (positivistic) in outlook, not really allowing for a mix of a more formal teaching style and something more spontaneous, which is the usual way schools work. Although he does mention one teacher's solitary attempt to move beyond the "drudgery" of normal lessons, trying to develop in students a more critical stance (McLaren 1993: 218). Moving forward in time to the present-day situation in Poland and more engaged / engaging educational practices, a debate continues over the professed aims of education and what is actually delivered in schools, especially relevant in light of recent reforms. One example of this can be seen in the concerns of articles appearing in the journal *Problemy Wczesnej Edukacji / Issues in Early Education*, e.g. Magdalena Wawrzyniak-Śliwska (2007) who writes about the differences between what teachers believe and what they actually practise, and Józefa Bałachowicz (2009) who shows the discrepancies between the generally accepted aims for education and what is written in the curriculum.

in this particular process it is the individuals themselves who set the meaning of their world as it exists (Dembiński 2005: 38), with the surrounding world being created anew by the enactment of the ritual. Dembiński (2005: 56–59) also goes into some detail about what the **co-celebrants** of this knowledge might experience, when he recounts how the enactment of ritual is connected with "the social drama" and the "entry into the ritual". As far as Dembiński is concerned, the first of these includes the breaking of rules, crisis, a loss of balance, followed by reintegration or schism, the second stages of separation, marginalization and reintegration (van Gennap 2004), or alternatively, preliminal, liminal and postliminal stages (Turner 1991). As all of this is possible within a period of liminality, which I propose is an integral part of happening, it might be assumed that a number or all of these characteristics will also appear as part of the enactment of happening in school. Additionally, Dembiński similarly to McLaren, also refers to Turner's idea of contact between people in the liminal state as being either one of **communitas**, "a none structured community, where all the individuals are unified, similar to one another and carry out the ritual of the powers that be – an ordinary person being the leader of the ceremony" (Dembiński 2005: 61, translation – MB) (in the case of the school, the teacher), or **antistructure**, which is "the movement beyond social roles and the possibility of finding open form, meaning, action and so on […] [in which] objects […] become forms without content or forms which carry content" (Dembiński 2005: 61, translation – MB). With its possibilities for involvement, breaking down barriers between participants, and participants and audience, happening might be said to embody communitas. At the same time, being aware of the "disruptive" possibilities for happening, the state of antistructure would also appear to be a possible condition for happening.

Another aspect of ritual that Dembiński (2005: 39–42) offers, which is useful in trying to understand happening more fully in relation to education, is its structure. This is divided between overt and covert systems. And, in an arrangement that in part echoes the form of happening, the overt system contains teacher and pupils, treated as both subjects and objects, as well as, and importantly, space, time, rhythm, objects, gestures and speech. These structures, in turn, move between involvement that is either **indexed** or **symbolic**: indexed involvement includes elements of the social-cultural arena which are fixed or prescribed, whereas symbolic involvement includes all those elements which are less fixed or more creative. This division between the indexed and the symbolic also exists and provides important points of reference for the covert workings of ritual. Around the index core lie elements such as myth, metonymy and syntagma, while around the symbol core lie anti-myth, paradigm and metaphor. In addition to this, the index core elements are those "which offer one particular way of solving a problem, normally, already tried and tested by the group" (Dembiński 2005: 39–40, translation – MB). In contrast the symbol core elements "contain a many sided potential for solving the problem" (Dembiński 2005: 39, translation – MB). It might be speculated that happening opens up opportunities that go beyond the index core towards the symbol core and all the opportunities it offers for creativity.

Returning to McLaren and his descriptions of the verbal interactions that take place within the liminal, streetcorner state, they also offer up another perspective from which to view the limen: Basil Bernstein's (2003: 98–103) concepts of **restricted** and **elaborated codes**. With a restricted code, for example, meaning is implicit, conveyed through a narrow range of linguistic elements, where the lexis and structures used are known to listeners, and where extra information may be given by paralinguistic features, such as gesture and facial expression, rather than linguistically. It is also inclusive, belonging to a particular group of people, thereby reducing the need for speakers to verbalize their intent. An elaborated code, on the other hand, conveys ideas through a broader range of linguistic elements, where meanings are expanded and verbally explicit. And whereas a restricted code uses communal symbols known to a particular group, an elaborated code uses individualized / personal symbols, and speakers can modify their speech to fit the needs of their listeners. Meanwhile, in writing about the streetcorner state, McLaren (1993: 87) describes verbal communication between students which incorporate "greater instances of irregular speech […] (e.g. spontaneous and ejaculatory expressions of feelings and emotions)", and with which students "are better able to confront their emotions directly and have a greater opportunity to share their emotions with select friends and peers" (McLaren 1993: 88–89). This draws a picture of a richness of formulation and communication beyond purely the verbal but also one that is confined to a particular group, which is reminiscent of a restricted code use. In contrast to this, in the student state, there is a real sense that the students must plug into the rhythms of the school; the students more able (and willing) to do so being the ones who will be more successful. These students are also the ones who, coming from Azorean working-class families, have "mastered the art of 'acting middle-class'" (McLaren 1993: 119), which suggests that they have adopted an elaborated code which is more available to the middle-classes (Bernstein 2003: 117), as well as the embodied cultural capital that Bourdieu (2011: 83–84) outlines. Taking these points on board, it is fair to assume that the liminal space of happening in education will be open to participants using a restricted code and not just an elaborated code which is more usual for school.

This possibility to use everyday language is also important beyond the potential it offers for emotional expression, for, as Krystyna Ablewicz (1997: 20) has commented, the use of everyday language allows us to understand ourselves and the surrounding world, while Zdzisław Aleksander (1992: 242) writes that it also provides a means by which understanding between generations might (should) take place. Meanwhile, if we do not allow such expression in schools, there is a risk that we will forfeit the chance for mutual understanding, but even more debilitating, there will be a breakdown of meaningful communication altogether (Aleksander 1992: 243). In the liminal space of happening it can be surmised there will be an opportunity for participants to use everyday language that will facilitate communication and also a deeper understanding between the generations.

In addition to language codes, two other concepts provided by Bernstein (2003: 157–159), **classification** and **framing**, might usefully be considered in relation to the limen and happening. Classification refers to the strength of the boundaries between subject areas. With strong classification (collection code) there is a definite delineation between subjects. In contrast, when there is weak classification, the distinction between subjects becomes more blurred (which can be the case in the primary sector) (Bernstein (2003: 161), so that an integrated code is applied. Framing, meanwhile, relates to the amount of control teachers and pupils have over the choice and organization of their learning, as well as to the amount of knowledge to be presented and learned during the educational encounter. When there is strong framing, the teacher and learners have little control, with weak framing they have noticeably more. Moreover, when there is weak framing, teachers and pupils have opportunities to use their everyday knowledge to explore ideas and to help further their understanding.

With its integration of many forms of expression, happening does away with the boundaries between different arts and practices (see Chapter 2, section 2.3.1), so that multi-various forms and connections are sought and played out in its liminal space. This way of working transferred into an educational setting at the level of curriculum and in relation to Bernstein's conceptualization, would favour integrated code rather than collection code; that is weakly rather than strongly classified, where the borders between different areas of knowledge are less clearly defined, allowing for movement between them. Moreover, with reference to framing, because happening is positioned first and foremost in life (see Chapter 2, section 2.1), in an educational setting it can be expected to provide ample opportunities for teachers and learners to use their knowledge of the everyday world when tackling issues in school.

3.3.2. The teacher as a liminal servant

The greater possibilities for partnership that the liminal space of happening allows, which can be linked to educational practice through Bernstein's concept of framing: "the what" and "the how" of teaching and who has control over it, means that another type coined by McLaren now becomes relevant to a consideration of that liminal space: the teacher as a liminal servant. This is because, as McLaren describes her,[45] this kind of teacher listens to her students, is involved with them and works with them to try to create an educational environment that will not only help them to learn but also empower them as students and people. This teacher as a liminal servant might also provide clues as to the characteristics and involvement of the teacher involved in happening.

From an extensive list of characteristics for the teacher as a liminal servant provided by McLaren (1993: 114–117), the most salient emphasize the teacher's awareness of her students, her political-emancipatory conviction and the varying roles she adopts, as well as the risks that are involved.

Above all, the teacher as a liminal servant is aware of her students, which shows itself in the way she supports the learning process, both in terms of its content and affective features, as well as creating the conditions to facilitate it. This means that the teacher presents ideas that are relevant to her students and in a form that is understandable to them, while making sure that any barriers to learning are taken away. The teacher as a liminal servant also enjoys participating in the learning process along with her students, teaching "in order to discover meanings for herself, not because she wishes to share available answers" (McLaren 1993: 117). According to McLaren, the teacher as a liminal servant also understands her students and so adopts a more holistic approach to teaching, where there is no division between the emotional and rational, active and passive, but rather where these dualities are promoted as equally valid parts of the same learning process. With the latter this means the teacher helps to transform student consciousness by creating situations where they can embody knowledge, while the teacher herself moves away from simply presenting knowledge. In addition to these characteristics, McLaren (1993: 115–116) also sees the liminal servant as a teacher who adopts an empirical-theoretical stance; someone who relies upon observation and diagnosis, and who is not afraid to mix theory and intuition when it comes to making decisions or carrying out actions related to her teaching practice.

45 McLaren's teacher as a liminal servant is female and I maintain this convention throughout this part of my discussion.

As well as being a student-orientated practice that aims at sharing the teaching-learning process with the students, there is also a strong political-emancipatory side to the teacher as a liminal servant. For McLaren, this entails acknowledging that students come from different socio-cultural groupings, which, in turn, has a bearing upon their position within the classroom, school and education system as a whole, as well as within society more broadly. For the teacher as a liminal servant meanwhile, the inequalities that inevitably follow from these differences are challenged, being held up for critical inquiry as much as the content that is part of the curriculum. Indeed, as far as McLaren is concerned, the teacher as a liminal servant sees all her students as academically equal. Therefore, in this situation the teacher becomes "a convener of customs and a cultural provocateur [...] [who] does not subordinate the political rights of students to their utility as future members of the labour force. She is a social activist and spiritual director as much as a school pedagogue" (McLaren 1993: 115).

In this movement away from being simply a school pedagogue, the teacher as a liminal servant is also assigned a number of roles. Unsurprisingly, considering McLaren's indebtedness to Turner, the most prominent among these takes her away from being an "ideologue", placing her status on a par with "a shaman" or "a mystic", with the teacher performing "the rights of instruction" in a "holy-play". At one and the same time, McLaren also views the liminal servant teacher as a more ambiguous figure, able to utilize forms of consciousness stemming from both the male and female character. As well as this, there is something anti-hierarchical and anti-authority / anti-authoritarian about this kind of teacher, who is a "vagrant", a "symbol of demystifying conscientization", calling into question even the most ordinary things that surround us. Indeed, this questioning of already existing and accepted positions shows itself in an orientation that is both anti-structure and very structured, so that as McLaren (1993: 116) writes, the teacher as a liminal servant "does not put a high priority on structure and order (although her classes may be highly structured and ordered)".

If the teacher as a liminal servant offers possibilities for ways of being and forms of action open to the teacher involved in happening, then it also comes with a word of warning: according to McLaren the role of the liminal servant teacher, which involves critical awareness and the adoption of varied and sometimes contradictory functions, is prone to unpredictability, at times taking on a life of its own. It may also, as McLaren (1993: 117) ominously states "'blow up' in the teacher's face, leaving both teacher and students emotionally scarred". Overall, however, it is rewarding, as students working together with the liminal servant teacher:

- respond with a sense of immediacy and purpose to the teacher's performance, both with gesture and verbally;
- become primary actors;
- are engaged in the authentic ritual of instruction;
- become co-celebrants of knowledge with the teacher. (McLaren 1993: 113–114)

3.4. Concluding remarks

It is possible to place happening as a performative practice and heir to a democratic tradition in education that reaches back to the progressivism of Dewey and forward to the critical-emancipatory projects of the likes of Giroux and McLaren. It is also conceivable to view it as a practice which encourages active learner and teacher involvement that is peer based rather than teacher-led or dominated; one close in type to that offered by the teacher as a liminal servant operating within a symbolic rather than indexed order. In addition to this, happening is a form which affords options of learning from "the other" (Witkowski) or "the outsider" (Rutkowiak) and where subject-object relations are redefined to become subject-subject relations or, according to Domańska, freed up from these textual constraints altogether. As a result, happening in education can be a practice for change rather than the maintenance of an educational status quo and, beyond education, change in society itself.

In the following chapter, happening is placed in relation to a number of pedagogical models so as to situate it more firmly within existing educational discourses. In addition to this, happening-type practices are considered in two cycles of education: early education and secondary education, in a discussion of what it might have to offer the compulsory education system.

4. Happening into education

Happening has an artistic provenance because of which it can be assumed to be a creative enterprise. Additionally, as was outlined in Chapter 2, its ambivalent relationship with the theatre means that this particular connection needs to be considered with regard to happening as an educational practice. Therefore, these two areas form the starting point of an examination of happening and education in this chapter. To begin with, a comparison of happening with drama pedagogy will be made and then analysis in relation to two constructivist models of learning as well as creativity. Following this, the reception of creativity within Polish schools at the present time is studied as a point from which to view the (possible) reception of happening. Moreover, two forms of happening-type practice that have taken place recently, one in early education in Poland and the other in the secondary sector in America, are reviewed in terms of their application at those two levels of education respectively. Issues that arise from their use are also examined.

The scope of interest is necessarily wide in this chapter owing to the fact that happening is rare in school-based education in Poland. This also explains why the two practices analysed are from different stages of education and from different countries. As a result of this, rather than concentrating on one specific issue relating to happening in school or one particular level of education, the aim is to present **issues that will help elucidate how happening might operate in school based education** in Poland.

4.1. Happening in relation to drama pedagogy

In Chapter 2, it was shown how a number of commentators locate happening in a theatrical tradition and although it is difficult to categorize it as purely entertainment, it does lean in that direction in some of its incarnations. In other happenings, however, it appears to fit more comfortably into a tradition of theatre whose aim is to effect transformations. In order to gauge more fully how happening might operate in an educational setting, a comparison to drama in education will now be made in order to highlight similarities and differences.

According to Maria Królica (2006), who has analysed both drama and happening in relation to early education, both forms share certain characteristics. For instance, they offer ways of organizing the learner's experience, as well as the educational space, in relation to the tasks they are involved in and the different props and materials which are used. This variety also stimulates creativity in the learner, while, at the same time, freeing her/him from external forms of control, or a system of assessment that only rewards "the right way of doing things". Moreover, both methods can be used to awaken the imagination and sensitivity of learners, as well as their ability to concentrate and a sense of discipline (Królica 2006: 51). Królica also proposes other benefits. Each method gives learners the possibility to become aware of their own thinking processes, of problems and problem solving and, through work in groups and involvement in various types of interaction, the creation of norms for themselves and the group. Throughout their preparation and enactment, drama and happening are also seen by Królica (2006: 100) to be of benefit because of the broad spectrum of emotions they allow learners to experience. Indeed, in connection with pre-school children, Królica is full of praise for both methods in relation to the effects they can achieve. This is because learners who have been involved in either drama and happening are

> more active, tolerant, confident, inquisitive, show greater self-confidence, friendliness, have a feeling of agency (they are aware that they themselves are responsible for what happens), concentration of attention, expressiveness, emotionality, are open to act together, and create a more cohesive group. (Królica 2006: 101, translation – MB)

However, even though there are points of similarity in relation to the types of stimulation and freedom both methods offer: the opportunities they provide for cognitive and emotional development, as well as socialization, there are differences between the way that happening *may* be constructed and the way that drama *is* constructed, which must, I believe, make a difference in the way that the participants are involved. The reasons for these differences can be related to a number of happening's characteristics outlined in Chapter 2: compartmentalization, the element of chance (and the implications it holds for the relation of happening to real life and the part fiction plays), the use of role, and on from that, the form of participation it calls for. In trying to distinguish between drama and happening further, the major attributes of drama in education as noted by Krystyna Pankowska will be looked at in comparison to happening. In doing so, reference will also be made to the work of Katarzyna Krasoń and her considerations of conventional theatre and the construction of fiction and role.

As Pankowska describes it, in drama used in education, similar to traditional drama, "The building of the action […] always has a dynamic character. Five phases can be identified: **exposition, development,** the **culminating point**, **vicissitudes** and the **resolution** (the ending)" (Pankowska 2000: 116, translation – MB). In comparison, happening based upon **compartmentalization** *does not* have to be involved in this scheme. Therefore, there does not have to be exposition which sets up a situation that demands further development. Neither do the action and the different scenes in happening have to be joined in any way or comment upon each other in a narrative development. They can simply co-exist, either simultaneously or linearly, being self-contained elements of a whole that do not have to move towards any sort of culmination, nor away from it, into an exploration of the vicissitudes that follow. There does not have to be any form of resolution either. Additionally, with compartmentalization, a happening may start and/or end with any particular action or non-action, as is wished.[46] Indeed, as Pawłowski (1982: 30, translation – MB) states, "the various compartments of happening, and this applies equally to those that are organized simultaneously as well as sequentially, can be organized in any order, left out or added, without affecting the structure".

Looking at the element of **chance**, Pankowska (2000: 128–129, translation – MB) writes that drama

> does not depend on the "playing" of something prepared, written in a script in terms of words and a situation. It is always something improvised, created as it occurs, constantly modified, and reliant upon relations with other characters who also undergo modification, similar to the course of the whole drama. [...] [And where] Often in the process of one drama session a number of versions of the same character will appear.

To all intents and purposes then, in drama, it is in the interaction between characters where chance operates, where relations between people are not always foreseeable or controllable and where a script, or more likely a general outline of events, giving an overall direction to the drama, might only be known to the person leading the group.

In contrast to how chance exists in drama, Pawłowski gives an idea of how it can exist in happening. And here he does not place emphasis solely on the interaction between the participant-actors, but includes a number of constituents that are part of the happening: the audience-participants, the compartments, and the actions and objects (Pawłowski 1982: 30). Indeed, as Pawłowski would have it, chance in happening becomes the guiding principle even taking over the function of storyline:

> the choice of objects and participants in happening, as well as their relations to one another, the organization of space and time, their behaviour, use of light and sound – all of these are not meant to be given meaning through story, [...] through the relation of

46 This can be seen most fully, for instance, in those happenings which adhere to compartmentalization as the basis for their structure, such as Kaprow's first happening, *18 Happenings in 6 Parts* (1959), Oldenburg's *Gayety* (1963) or Kantor's *The Dividing Line* (1966).

means to an end, but should be a consequence of chance. (Pawłowski 1982: 31, translation – MB)

The way in which chance exists in happening also means that happeners can achieve another important goal: that of bringing **art closer to life**. Happeners feel this to be possible because taking away the idea of a story that can be followed or read by an audience makes happening closer to how real life actually operates: where events and actions which are not connected occur around us, and where there is no cause and effect inherent in their being – rather a storyline is something imposed by us or someone else. This does not mean that happenings have not been scripted – they have, and in some cases these scripts have been followed quite closely.[47] The scripts of happening, however, are not something that have followed the more conventional form of traditional drama where spoken exchanges between characters are given which develop its five phases. Happening scripts are, and have been, more an attempt to "choreograph" the different compartments and events of the happenings, giving more emphasis to the actions to be carried out, objects to be used, timing and so on. In one sense, they might be seen to be closer to the stage directions which appear in a more traditional script, in another they could be regarded as a form of poetic text which guides but does not control the enactment of the happening.[48] With this situation, another difference between drama and happening also opens up, and that is the way they are each involved with **fiction**. For Pankowska (2000: 137, translation – MB), for example, fiction helps us make sense of the world, and by extension, "The activity of drama is one which creates meaning, and through

---

47 Kaprow began by trying to keep quite strictly to a script which, in itself, involved a great deal of rehearsal time. As he went on, however, and time became less available, the scripts became much simpler and more negotiated with the participants, so that "Those who wished to participate could decide for themselves" (Kirby 1966: 49). Kaprow also seems to sum up the situation for most happeners in relation to how tightly a performance is bound by its script. He writes: "Obviously things are done variously and flexibly in the actual performance. There are the contributions of each person, the accidents of weather, the slips in timing, etc., which nobody can figure on. Sometimes they are marvellous, sometimes not. I allow for this. I try to plan for different degrees of flexibility within parameters of an otherwise strictly controlled imagery" (Kirby 1966: 51).

48 Robert Whitman's working procedure on *The American Moon* consisted of a mixture of words and pictures, as well as "suggestions", negotiated throughout the process of producing the happening, rather than fixed and determined points to be accomplished at all costs (Kirby 1966: 137). Klara Kemp-Welch (2006: 46–47) talks about the "unconventional poetic system of writing" that Kantor used as the basis for his happenings.

which we give sense to our life". Vital to this enterprise too, as far as Krasoń is concerned, are the actors, who, in conventional theatre, construct a theatrical present, where each actor

> takes on the task given to him by the creator of the stage production, a task which conditions the generation of actions by the actor, either active or verbal behaviour, which, at the same time, plainly signal that they are determined by the world that is being symbolized. (Krasoń 2013: 88, translation – MB)

In happening, however, fiction does not have to play a part, it being closer to life than drama or conventional theatre. As a result of this, with happenings, there does not need to be fiction in the sense of something being constructed[49] or of actors being involved at all. As Kaprow (2003: 195) writes, "It [happening] was the difference between watching an actor eating strawberries on stage and actually eating them yourself at home. **Doing life** [my emphasis – MB]".

To gain a better understanding of what "doing life" might mean in comparison to the fiction in drama, it is useful here to look more closely at three features for drama that Pankowska gives, and then consider how happening "deviates" from them. Pankowska (2000: 143) states that the fiction in drama is based upon the following:

49 Pawłowski comments upon this when he considers the structure of more traditional forms of art in relation to the structure of happening: "In a great many traditional works of art, such as drama, film, and novels – the connections between the parts are a result of the story arising between them in terms of their logic and causal nature. These connections create an information structure, joining the separate pieces into one whole. This information structure then permits an understanding of the characters, as well as the motives for their actions, placing the events presented in a logical progression. Happening does not have such an information structure: it is made up of isolated and independent parts, so called compartments or events. Between the compartments of happening there is no sharing of information, as occurs, for example, in traditional theatre, where one part prepares the way for the next or explains the event occurring earlier" (Pawłowski 1982: 27, translation – MB). In continuing with his description of its structure, Pawłowski also comments upon the place real life can have in happening, taking us to the extremes of what the form can offer: "A number of happeners are even more radical. They not only eliminate story but also state that happening should not fulfil any mimetic function, present anything, or symbolize or mean anything. It should rather be real activity, taking place amongst real objects, similar to what takes place within everyday life" (Pawłowski 1982: 27–28, translation – MB).

- common sense, where what is contained in the drama is, in some way true, or relatively true in relation to the participants' cognitive experiences;
- the ordering of the material, which will be in accordance with accepted ideas (philosophy, historical, ethical and so on), as well as being connected to the author's vision, allowing her/him to combine the elements in an unexpected way, different from the usual set of socially accepted stereotypes;
- acceptance of the conventional norms established in classic drama, where everything proceeds in a series of small steps towards the creation of the conflict, the building of the tension / suspense, through to the resolution of the action.

The first two features could also take into account the fiction of happening, with the caveat that happening might push each of them to an extreme position.[50] With the third feature, however, except for those happenings which are closer to traditional theatre, two of the main characteristics possible for happening itself, compartmentalization and the non playing of role, do not permit the procedure outlined above. This is because they do not allow for the sequencing of action nor the psychical (intrapersonal) and social (interpersonal) interaction that are an integral part of drama. As a result of this, there can be no building of **tension** and suspense towards a state of **conflict** which might then be resolved as, according to Pankowska (2000: 154, translation – MB), conflict arises from people (actors) engaged in fulfilling their own particular needs or clashing over differences and values that occur because of their group status.

As the significance of compartmentalization for happening in comparison to the way that drama is structured has been analysed, the significance of the exclusion of role in happening will now be looked at. In relation to the chance and conflict within drama, **role** is seen to be vitally important. Indeed, Pankowska goes as far as to place it as *a*, if not *the* prime motivator behind the development of the whole drama:

> Role is very often dependent upon the way in which the other characters in the drama are portrayed. Its creation must take place within the context of the other characters, and especially those with whom it has immediate contact. Only when there is this mutual

50 In Kantor's *Panoramic Sea Happening*, for example, participant-audience credulity may have been tested by female bodies writhing in a mixture of tomato ketchup and sand. In Kaprow's *A Spring Happening*, meanwhile, the audience was "attacked" by a lawnmower. Similarly, Orange Alternative's happening on the eve of the 70th anniversary of the Russian Revolution (6 November, 1987), must have caused great consternation: its overt support of the anniversary was also a form of opposition to the communist regime.

dependence of roles is the full structure of the drama created. (Pankowska 2000: 129, translation – MB)

And, again, Krasoń provides a fuller picture when she writes about conventional theatre and how the construction of role is intimately tied up with the fiction that is set in place. Thus, in creating a character, the actor has the choice of two strategies: either she/he can dress "her/himself in a second skin, an organic mask", or use the "stage character like a trampoline, enabling her/him to go deeper into what is hidden behind the mask of daily life" (Krasoń 2013: 80–81, translation – MB). This does not have to be the case with happening, however, where, because of compartmentalization, dependency on other people or fiction is limited: there does not have to be any form of communication nor connection between participants exploring a story, neither do they have to develop any form of relationship that will lead to the development of the happening itself.[51]

In considering role further, Pankowska (2000: 134, translation – MB) also comments that both drama and theatre "try to create a deeper understanding of life in society, a life that is most often reflected in the different roles people take on or which they are given. In their own lives in society, people are fathers, teachers, wives, superiors and so on". This understanding of the roles people play in "real life" and not just the different stereotypes which are offered generally, is one of the aims of drama (Pankowska 2000: 135). Happening's involvement in role, however, would appear to be even more fundamental: closer to real life. As a result, happening is not so much bothered with finding out "the truth" of what lies behind these particular roles, but more to create an understanding that these often "givens" of society are indeed roles, and that we do have some influence over how they might be played out.[52] Indeed, this is something which comes closer to the efficacious function of theatre discussed in Chapter 2 (section 2.1), and, as we have seen above, one of the possibilities for the actor working with

51 Connections may be made by the participants and people watching, but these may not necessarily be intentional. A condition which appears to be upheld by Kaprow's pronouncement that as far as he was concerned, his first happening would have no meaning (Chapter 2, section 2.1.1.1).

52 This relates to the critical and emancipatory possibilities of happening mentioned in Chapter 2, sections 2.3.2.4 and 2.4.1: the Orange Alternative happening of June 1988, where calling for the police disempowers it as a force to be afraid of; the young mother for whom Orange Alternative happenings had a sociotherapeutical function, allowing her to step outside of her situation and view it from a different perspective; and, Strefa Ciszy's *Postscriptum*, which posed a question to the idea of relationship formation in consumerist society through the sale of male companions.

role that Krasoń mentions; where the stage character is used as a trampoline for a deeper exploration of society as a whole. In this way, then, it is possible to say that drama is more concerned with interpretation and understanding, whereas happening is more about emancipation and empowerment.

Finally, another difference between happening and drama also reveals itself in the area of role and its wider implication for participation. There is an assumption underlying the use of drama in education that there is someone, one person, overseeing and guiding the whole process:

> In the creation of role the leader plays an unusually important part. As it is she/he – knowing the purpose of the project and being aware of its aims – who will pay attention to all of the most important elements, in relation to the other characters and their functions, and within the whole context of the drama. It is the leader, after all, who is aware of what she/he wants to achieve in the drama, through the given roles. In this situation she/he becomes a selector: choosing one possible interpretation from among the great many available. These choices being made at every stage of the drama. (Pankowska 2000: 132, translation – MB)

This deference to a "higher authority" is against the possibility I suggest is available to happening, with its preference for more equal and active participation from all those people involved in its proceedings.

Summing up, it would appear that happening allows participants to take one step further back from their involvement in the action than drama, so that the processes involved and the parts participants play in them are opened up even more. As a result of this, in comparison with drama, happening offers something that

- is closer to real life because it does not try to tie things together in a complete and purposeful whole, to impose meaning, for example, at the level of cause and effect;
- allows participants to interact openly and freely with the surrounding environment, people and objects;
- offers freedom from norms imposed by the form itself;
- allows participants to be themselves as they are involved in a particular activity or action, or have a greater awareness of themselves taking on a role demanded by an activity or action;
- provides participants with an opportunity to share responsibility for what they are doing – with no ultimate authority guiding the action or even knowing where it will eventually lead.

This would appear to have significance for happening in education in terms of school, because if it can be said that drama has made a place for itself within school, it is now time for happening to do so. All the more so, because as described in the first three chapters, happening has strong connections with the cultural climate within which we all live (including the young generation that is involved in schooling): one which is postmodern, chaotic and unstable, and where participatory democracy is promoted. In relation to this, therefore, it would seem that the use of happening in school would help learners engage with this world in their education. In doing so, it would also have implications across three main areas in relation to schooling:

- the way that people engage with knowledge, the processes of education, and
- the way they are involved with school, the place in which they gain that knowledge.

These, in turn, would also impact on

- how people participate.

4.2. Happening – engagement and creativity

Generally, the use of happening in school would challenge the way in which it (school) traditionally functions in terms of its educational processes and its surroundings. At the various stages of a happening's production, for example, it can be assumed that it will provide alternative opportunities relating to the way that people engage with knowledge, how they participate, either individually or together, and how they are involved in the space of school itself. In addition to this, there is a strong creative strand underlying happening which needs to be considered in relation to educational practice and which is not usually supported or even given a chance to exist in Polish schools.

4.2.1. Engagement with knowledge

In terms of how people engage with knowledge, in the planning and preparation of the happening, participants would have the opportunity to discuss issues and topics relevant to their own interests and situations, which might then become the basis for further action or for the happening itself. This would make it similar to the project method in that the initiative for ideas and action come from the learners and teachers, or even other people (Szymański 2010: 77), and not from a set of formulaic ways of thinking and procedures (pp. 92–93). And, as with the project method, everyone (learners and teacher) would be involved in this in equal measure, so that

> It is not important from whom the initiative comes, it is important that there is an overall climate of spontaneity, a willingness to act, as well as to get to know something new. Meanwhile, the proposal itself does not bind anyone to anything, as during the course of the discussion it might be accepted or rejected. (Szymański 2010: 77–78, translation – MB)

Applied to happening, this focus on individual interests and needs, as well as working with others to decide upon and develop ideas in an atmosphere of lively interest and acceptance, would place it in a therapeutic model of education; where the affective factors attendant on the educational process are as important as the cognitive ones (Gołębniak 2007: 111).

In addition to this choice over content, there are also implications arising from the characteristics of happening that have an impact upon how learners and teachers are involved with knowledge and how learners gain understanding. If during the happening, for example, the learners and teacher are involved in connecting its various elements, making sense of the whole, this would situate it in an educational constructivist paradigm. Moreover, depending on how the learners and teacher work together, this might be one of two forms of that paradigm, or a movement between the two. It could be the more challenging **developmental constructivist model**, where, as Klus-Stańska (2009: 61, translation – MB) describes it, "Learning is presented as active and exploratory, as well as independent in terms of the conceptual and decisive construction and reconstruction of the mind's model of reality". It is also a continuous process where both the learner and the teacher are involved in equal measure in creating meaning (Klus-Stańska 2009: 61). The other form of constructivism that might be adopted is less demanding on the learner at an individual level and also privileges the teacher as someone who knows more, and therefore can help the learner towards understanding. In this **social constructivist model**,

> the child is treated as less independent and self-sufficient than in developmental-constructivist discourse. His general knowledge, gained in spontaneously initiated and realized experimental procedures without the involvement of adults, is not enough [...] to build accurate or [even] adequate knowledge. From this it follows that a fundamental condition for successful learning is with the teacher's support (although not through transmission and instruction). (Klus-Stańska 2009: 66, translation – MB)

In the most up to date form of social constructivism, meanwhile, the relationship in the creation of meaning (learners – learners; learners – teacher) is one of equals, where a procedure of joint negotiation is emphasized (Klus-Stańska 2009: 67–68). It would seem likely, therefore, that in carrying out happening there would be an adoption of one of these forms of constructivism, or a movement between the two, depending on the age and needs of the learners, how the teacher perceives her/his own role in best serving those learners, and the purpose and stages of the happening. Needless to say, a familiarity with such educational models, as well as a willingness to implement them, would also apply here (Klus-Stańska 2009: 67–68).

Moving to the stages of a happening's production, in its preparation and presentation, there are also opportunities to work in different media, which is readily pointed out by Królica (2006: 47). These different media could range from sound and music to the visual and the plastic arts, including more physically expressive forms such as movement and dance (see Chapter 2, section 2.1, for a broad range of activities advocated for happening by Kaprow). Additionally, the fact that objects are an integral part of happening means learners could be involved in choosing them, or, if they are to be made, designing and constructing them. There would also be potential for manipulating these objects throughout the different stages of the happening, and not only in ways that are originally intended.

Overall, therefore, there is a creativity inherent to happening that includes the way that participants are involved in choosing ideas and linking them together, the range of expressive means available and contact with objects. Furthermore, because there are demands on the teacher and pupils to work together in various ways: bringing together ideas and discussing them, working with a number of expressive means and formulating a variety of concepts and opinions, a selection of different and constantly changing interaction patterns would be necessary. This, in turn, would entail the use of different spatial arrangements around the classroom (or other spaces) throughout the different stages of production (and enactment) of the happening.

A comparison with the project method is again informative here, where, according to Mirosław Szymański (2010: 79–84), general organizational matters, as well as those relating to the particular aim of a project, are all taken as a whole – as an integral part of the project in hand. Here, too, there is an understanding that the participants in a project will be meeting in different formations throughout its realization, which Szymański (2010: 77, translation – MB), citing Carl Frey, calls "team-time" and "meta-interaction". In terms of happening, it is envisaged that participants would be involved in its organization, as well as in a consideration of its content. They would also either work individually, in pairs, in smaller or larger groups, or as a whole class. Additionally, as was mentioned above, they would use different areas of the classroom: desks and tables, the floor, the walls, or even go beyond the classroom, away from the school altogether.

All of this is a far remove from forms of school instruction in which the teacher as an authority transmits information to pupils. Here there is much more interaction, with both teachers and learners engaged with one another, different forms of expression and various objects, embarking on a journey in which the final destination (outcomes) cannot, perhaps even should not, be determined from the start if it is to retain its creative character. Fulfilment of this **emancipatory aspect of happening**, of course, does rely upon the willingness of teachers (the school) to be involved in such an enterprise. This would mean, for example, that the element of chance is allowed and the lesson plan is set aside in favour of a more spontaneous, open and mutual involvement with learners; where, after Klus-Stańska (2002), there is a willingness to let learners "search for a path" rather than simply make them follow one. Whether or not Polish school, steeped in a tradition of transmission based teaching, is ready for this is something that will now be considered. In doing so, the creative aspect of happening will be concentrated upon and, on from that, how creativity is received in Polish schools generally.

4.2.2. Creativity and school

Involvement in happening places requirements upon all those participating very similar to the ones Krzysztof J. Szmidt describes for engagement in creativity, all of which are important attributes for an emancipatory practice. Szmidt (2007: 51, translation – MB) writes that creativity

> demands from the creator both **involvement** and **independence** [my emphasis throughout – MB], the creation of solutions and – at the same time – their assessment, it is not the same as intelligence but neither is it specifically that different, it demands deep knowledge but also **freedom from its limitations**, it can mean the making of something new, but can also be researched without being linked to a product [...], it demands the **overstepping of social norms**, but is also **tolerated by society**.

Echoing Szmidt's ideas, Anna Sajdak (2008: 42–60) outlines what can be expected from an appropriate creative educational environment. Firstly, Sajdak states that it should allow for **autonomy** and **freedom**, so that the person involved in the creative process feels she/he can explore and find alternatives rather than search for the one and only, "right" answer. On from this, according to Sajdak, autonomy also refers to the fact that learners should be **encouraged to formulate their own aims** for carrying out tasks and helped in fulfilling them. What is more, they should also be motivated to continue in their research once they have completed their initial inquiry. Finally, Sajdak equates creative education to **a meeting with other people, their views and experiences,** which – at a fundamental level – means a relationship between teachers and learners where they are willing to share and learn from one another. This would appear to correspond with the possibilities offered by happening as outlined above. It is also a dynamic and open structure in relation to creativity which is upheld by Edward Nęcka.

Representing the interactive school of thinking in psychology, Nęcka (1994: 20–22) believes that creativity is a continuous and reciprocal process of two elements working together: (a) the aim of the creative activity, and (b) the structure that is revealed through the different trials that are carried out in trying to reach that aim. Moreover, the trials themselves might also have an effect upon the original aim, modifying it with each new piece of information that is received while being involved in the trial itself. In such a situation, the difference between the trial and the aim steadily diminishes until a final aim is realized. In addition, as Nęcka would have it, such an interaction is due to a specific creative strategy: the cognitive operations of the "maker-doer", as well as critical thinking. Meanwhile, in such a situation, there is an inherent flexibility and responsiveness that does not aim at a pre-determined fixed point on behalf of the creator but rather involvement in a process that is modified (refined) as it is in motion, open to and, more importantly, responsive to, new stimuli at every step along its path. Nęcka also provides a model of creativity which is useful to refer to in connection with happening as it gives ideas of the various types of involvement that might be expected from people.

In his model, Nęcka (1994: 21) outlines three different criteria from which to view creativity:

- the characteristics of the product created,
- the characteristics of the thought processes involved,
- the psychological reaction of the recipients.

Of these, elements of the second and third are perhaps the most relevant for viewing the creativity of happening in terms of cognitive processes.

In relation to Nęcka's outline of the process of thinking involved in creative processes, it might be envisaged that the participants in a school happening (pupils and teacher) will show **activeness**, as they will display elements of spontaneity and flexibility in their thinking. They will also have an **active involvement with the material,** willing to change the aim of their activities in the course of pursuing them. In addition to this, and in terms of what Nęcka calls **synthesis**, participants will also be able to connect up ideas and facts into new and intelligible wholes, even those which from the outset might appear irreconcilable. Nęcka's model also provides indicators of the reactions to expect from those people who are involved in or come into contact with the happening. In terms of the psychological reaction of the recipient or audience in contact with creativity, Nęcka (1994: 20, translation – MB) refers to the mixtures of "shock and acceptance" or "surprise and agreement" that contact with creativity might draw from those involved, and which Nęcka names **"effective" surprise**. There might also be an **initial mistrust** towards the creative act (happening), later to be followed by acceptance, or a process of **reassessment**, where the participants re-evaluate their first impressions of a particular experience. In addition to this, complementary reactions are possible relating to the perceived novelty of the happening or the fact that it is something the recipients themselves believe they might have done– **"I never would have thought of that"** and **"That's exactly what I would have done"** (Nęcka 1994: 21, translation – MB).

The possibility for creativity within education (and therefore happening) does, however, rely upon a supportive atmosphere, which, unfortunately, does not always exist. In connection with this, and in general terms, Nęcka describes a number of **obstacles to creativity** within schools. For example, teachers can **limit the agency of learners** (Nęcka 1999: 164–168) by the way they view or react to creativity. They might not be creatively involved themselves and, because of this, be less inclined to promote it in their learners. Further, they might **punish creative reactions** which are interpreted as insubordination, leading to a situation where the spontaneous questions asked by learners are more likely to be seen as a nuisance rather than a sign of creative interest. In addition to this, teachers can have an **instrumental attitude**, which means learners never really have an opportunity to become involved creatively, as such activity is always *en route* to the fulfilment of another aim, rather than an end in itself.

Continuing Nęcka's ideas concerning the negation of creativity, it is possible for it to be limited because of **mental inertia** (Nęcka 1999: 175–178), where only one way of doing things is seen to exist, or because of the **prominence of a particular schema** (Nęcka 1999: 178–183), usually imposed on the younger generation by the older. This conservatism can also be responsible for interrupting creativity, where as part of a **prevailing dogmatism**, it does not allow it to develop (Nęcka 1999: 147). Interestingly, too, in terms of the possibilities for people working together in happening, Nęcka (1999: 158–161) sees **peer pressure** and the **conformism** it engenders as another factor that can interfere with the creativity of learners. **Rivalry** can also block creativity, especially when it is too strong between individuals, so that it becomes an end in itself rather than as part of the pursuit of a greater project (Nęcka 1999: 161–164).

Klus-Stańska also puts forward reasons why creativity might be hindered or blocked. In Polish schools especially, in terms of how they view creativity and the role that teachers can play, she sees the major problem being the still **heavy reliance upon a behaviouristic model** in teaching, as well as the forms of thinking and thereby practices it allows (Klus-Stańska 2006: 60–61). In addition to this, the **climate for creativity within school is severely limited** (Klus-Stańska 2006: 63–68) for fear of upsetting the status quo. As a result, the forms of creativity which are acceptable are the *ludic*, where the learner is allowed and encouraged to think in hypothetical ways, as long as it is within the realm of fantasy and the fantastic, or the *aesthetic*, in which the learner takes on the more stereotypical creative roles assigned by society, and more usually those of the plastic artist or the writer. In terms of the learner as *researcher* or *reformer*, which are the other two creative forms Klus-Stańska outlines, she believes the chances of them being encouraged, or even allowed, are extremely limited. In connection with the learner as researcher, this is because Polish education is still strongly grounded in the transmission model, where research by learners is used to verify what the teacher has already presented. This is different to a true spirit of inquiry, where the learner relies upon her/his own thinking, or as Klus-Stańska so aptly puts it, carries out experimentation as a "doubting Thomas". Indeed, Klus-Stańska (2002: 221–252, translation – MB) gives a series of empirically supported examples of how creativity in learners "in search of their own path" is blocked by teacher based practices at primary level, in favour of transmission orientated teaching, "following a given path". Finally, if the climate of learner as researcher is officially accepted by schools but not practised, the learner as reformer, according to Klus-Stańska (2006: 67–68), is rejected outright. This is because schools promote an adaptive form of socialization, where there is no place for resistance but rather obedience and subservience.[53]

If Klus-Stańska's diagnosis is correct, the full extent of creativity that happening promises may not be fulfilled. The aesthetic possibilities (see Chapter 2, section 2.3.2), for example, would be allowed, but the critical would have little or no chance of being accepted. In addition to what Klus-Stańska has to say about the socialization that occurs within schools, it is also important to bear in mind Marzena Nowicka's (2009: 265, translation – MB) description of Polish schools generally and the form of socialization that is prevalent, where "the imperative of finding **'the one right answer'** [my emphasis – MB], the rewarding of obedience

53 Klus-Stańska writes that the learner as researcher is accepted at an official level but does not appear in schools, whereas the learner-transformer is simply not to be imagined. As far as Klus-Stańska is concerned, this is a contradiction. She cannot understand why the constructive and reforming spirit that informs the possibilities of the learner-reformer in school is not allowed, when it can help the development of so many traits that are prized by society itself, where "Offering resistance is connected with striving towards autonomy, a talent for making independent decisions, a feeling of agency, as well as responsibility and courage" (Klus-Stańska 2006: 67, translation – MB).

and subordination, the standardization of points of view, the silencing of critical voices, the marginalization of individual needs and problems" are the norm. Additionally, summing up the results of empirical research carried out in early education, she comments that even "Social roles are presented to the child as a task to recreate and not create something, without the possibility of their negotiation" (Nowicka 2010: 387, translation – MB).

This all appears to be a far cry from the type of creative involvement that Szmidt mentions and Sajdak translates into an educational setting, and one which I suggest lies at the heart of happening as an educational enterprise. To paraphrase Szmidt in terms of happening in education, is "the society of school" willing or even able to have *its* "social norms" overstepped?

4.3. Happening in early education

In early education at present, the term *happening* is used to denote two forms of involvement. The most widespread, if the websites of various schools are looked at, is used to describe those events or occasions within the life of the school that are more than usual day-to-day classroom practice. This, however, covers a very broad a range of activities, so that it might be used to refer to the presentation of a drama, an exhibition of children's work or an organized visit to a particular place, such as a museum or zoo, or even a visitor to the school itself. And, while there is no denying that each of these activities might involve the individual in particular learning processes and promote creativity, they are not strictly happening, and so do not allow the realization of happening's potential in an educational setting. For this, and in relation to education in Poland, one must turn to Królica working with pre-school children in Częstochowa.

Królica (2006) sees the characteristics of happening as an attractive proposal for teachers who want to engage their students actively in the educational process. The different characteristics of happening within the context of education allow children to get in touch with their own creativity, to discover their own ways of interacting with other people and the world in general. Most importantly, however, as Królica believes, it frees children from a schematic way of behaving, while strengthening their feelings of responsibility for their actions. In particular, Królica (2006: 51, translation – MB) emphasizes that the experiences which lie at the foundation of happening, "sensitize to the affairs of everyday life, and not through instilling a stiff set of rules but rather through the emotional sensitivity that art shapes".

This idea of creative involvement as a form of introduction to the greater world and the need for the child to be involved in less schematic situations is echoed in the thinking of Hanna Krauze-Sikorska when she writes about artistic creation in the child. For Krauze-Sikorska (2006: 206, translation – MB), creative workshops provide a space where children are helped in the development of cognitive processes beyond ready-made ideas and, importantly, "without expectations of continuous inspiration from an adult". Overall, involvement in the plastic arts allows the child to gain a broad knowledge and set of ideas relating to reality as well as an opportunity to order that knowledge. Indeed, her research findings show that the child is able to analyze, compare and generalize more successfully after being involved in creative situations that allow her/him to do so. Such children are also able to bring a fuller store of ideas and more precision to their definitions and, in connection with this, their ways of thinking. As a result, as far as Krauze-Sikorska (2006: 200–202) is concerned, involvement in creative activities prepares the child for the more difficult tasks of distinguishing characteristics that are less obvious or totally abstract. She also sees involvement in artistic activities as prompting **multisensory cognition**, which helps the child develop towards more abstract levels of thinking with greater success (Krauze-Sikorska 2006: 199). Królica, meanwhile, believes the multisensory engagement that happening affords, through the use of movement, gesture, colour and sound, to be of great importance for early education, because in addition to intellectual development, it also helps in the physical and motor development of the child (Królica 2006: 51).

In connection with this, Howard Gardner's theory of **multiple intelligences** also appears relevant, not least because of the possibilities Gardner sees art offering education in relation to didactics. Gardner's (1999: 278)

> theory posits a small set of human intellectual potentials [...] of which all individuals are capable by virtue of their membership in the human species. Owing to heredity, early training, or, in all probability, a constant interaction between these factors, some individuals will develop certain intelligences far more than others; but every normal individual should develop each intelligence to some extent, given but a modest opportunity to do so.

These intelligences include the **linguistic, musical, logical-mathematical, visual-spatial, bodily-kinaesthetic, intrapersonal,** and **interpersonal.**[54] Additionally, in terms of their educational application, Gardner suggests five different ways of presenting themes, ideas or problems in education that will

54 There are others that have been discussed, such as naturalist, spiritual and existential. At the moment, Gardner believes there is a case for a naturalist intelligence (Gardner et al 2009: 6).

allow people with different intelligences to tackle them. These "points of entry", as Gardner labels them, appeal to a mixture of the different intelligences, so that whereas the narrational is primarily linguistically based, the aesthetic is a combination of the visual-spatial and musical-rhythmical intelligences. Other entry points include the logical-quantitative, the fundamental and the experiential-experimental. Significantly, Iwona Czaja and Monika Nęcka (2010: 193, translation – MB) believe that the latter entry point allows the child to experience "hands on contact with materials, action, construction and active involvement in projects and experiments, based above all on the kinaesthetic and interpersonal intelligences". Moreover, and importantly, in terms of the aims of this inquiry, one of the didactic methods they see as a useful exponent of this particular entry point is happening (Czaja and Nęcka 2010: 193).

In addition to the above, the emphasis on process in Gardner's model, where students learn through taking part in what interests them (which, in Gardner's case, means their predisposition in a particular field), is something Królica (2006: 51) stresses when she writes that the actual "solving" of the problem set by the happening is not important, but rather the act of taking part, of being involved in the action, "here and now". The broad range of subjects Królica is able to explore using happening also points to the fact that as a method in early education it is not only able to respond to individual learners' needs but also to those of the preschool curriculum, a situation which is borne out by the wide variety of subjects covered in the happenings Królica has carried out with preschoolers.[55]

Returning once again to Gardner and the multiple intelligences, there also appears to be a connection between the aims for his project as a whole, and what Królica envisages for happening. For Gardner, in accordance with the reading by Czaja and Nęcka (2010: 195), the educational process is very much linked to its usefulness to society, preparing the individual for their future life as an adult. Similarly, Królica sees the effects of happening not only applying to the present involvement of children but to the whole of their lives, as it "Allows children, and later adults, to orientate themselves in the world of things and objects" (Królica 2006: 51, translation – MB). The training which happening imparts, creating

55 The titles of some of the happenings Królica (2006: 123–136, translation – MB) has created and the areas in the programme they relate to are: *Water necessary to life* and *Let's become aware of the strength of the wind* – knowledge of the natural world; *Cleanliness is the basis of good health* – personal hygiene; *They cry rubbish!* – the environment; *Dangerous roads* and *Smoking cigarettes is our enemy* – health and safety; *Small aggressors* and *After losing a match* – society and behaviour, and *A knight's armour* and *The Polish family coat of arms* – history.

"a relation between these elements [which] allows for the treatment of the world of objects as the sum of human experience" (Królica 2006: 51, translation – MB). In this practical orientation, there is also a link with Dewey and his ideas about education (see Chapter 3, section 3.1.2.1). Indeed, Czaja and Nęcka trace the progressivist influence on Gardner, while their description of his school links it on a practical level to Dewey's ideas for how a school should operate.[56] Królica's reference to children finding themselves in the world of objects would also seem to recall the Dewey of the *Art of Experience*, and what Kruk mentions about the Deweyesque orientation towards objects, mentioned in Chapter 3 (section 3.2.4).

Finally, with regard to Gardner, there is, as Czaja and Nęcka (2010: 196) assert, a social dimension to his educational model, especially in its art orientation, which I believe chimes equally with Królica's ideas about involvement in happening, as well as Klus-Stańska's ideas for contemporary schooling (section 4.2.1 above). For all of them, learners actively work on tasks and problems in interaction with others, negotiating meanings and understandings. And indeed, with this emphasis on active engagement in problem solving and involvement with others, as well as the negotiation of meaning, which implies the use of language, these concerns lie at the heart of contemporary ideas about thinking and learning in relation to young learners, especially those based upon the research and findings of Jean Piaget, Lev Vygotsky and Jerome Bruner.

With specific reference to happening, for instance, and the possibilities it affords for "hands on" involvement in a number of different sensory areas, it would appear to offer ideal opportunities for what Piaget (Wood 1998: 5) calls active self-discovery, giving children the chance to construct meaning (knowledge) for themselves. In addition to these opportunities for cognitive development through action, there are also those afforded through the linguistic interaction between the children, which – as Piaget (Gross and Humphreys 1993: 765) and

56 In the Gardner school, for example, the day starts with the teaching of traditional subjects, although as Czaja and Nęcka (2010: 195, translation – MB) phrase it, "often in an untraditional way". This is then followed, in the second half of the day, by practical lessons, which are very often out of school under the tutelage of a teacher or an authority in the particular area of knowledge being presented. In *The School and Society*, Dewey (1956: 18) advocated the introduction of "active occupation" into schools, where learning takes place through "directed living", hands-on experience with materials and involvement with other people, instead of "abstract" and "remote" references, which Dewey saw as the usual lot of schools. In this instance, the Gardner school's involvement with people and institutions outside of the school would appear to be the next step on in terms of Dewey's hands-on experience.

other researchers believe – may help them to advance intellectually. The social and linguistic grounding of cognitive development, meanwhile, are taken even further by Vygotsky, and especially the role adults play, so that opportunities for "social interaction and such experiences as talking to, informing, explaining, being talked to, informed and having things explained, structure not only the child's immediate activities but also help to form the *processes* of reasoning and learning themselves" (Wood 1998: 135). In relation to Bruner (1983), in its planning, preparation and enactment, happening also offers the classroom teacher an additional format and routines within which language use, and through this cognitive growth, might take place. It is also a type of involvement where, with appropriate scaffolding (Wood 1998: 80) supplied by the teacher, the child might successfully work through a whole range of issues that are relevant to her/his situation as well as being part of the school curriculum.

As can be seen above, talk with others is of central importance in cognitive development. Its significance within an institutionalized educational environment, meanwhile, is considered in some detail by Douglas Barnes. Placing himself firmly in the constructivist tradition, Barnes (2010: 9) writes about opportunities to talk one's way into understanding in a form of engagement by learners he terms **"active learning"**. In such situations talking becomes a tool of thinking where new ideas can be discussed with fellow learners and teachers. In addition to this, Barnes (2010: 7) suggests other tools of thinking, such as the writing used in problem solving, the figures in mathematical problems or, in a form relevant to contemporary classroom practice, interactive whiteboards. Moreover, he also mentions tools which more readily call upon the possibilities inherent in happening, such as making drawings and diagrams or manipulating objects (Barnes 2008: 2). Ultimately, however, whatever tools are used, they are all modes of working on understanding which have at their core

> the idea of "trying out" new ways of thinking and understanding some aspect of the world: this trying out enables us to see how far a new idea will take us, what it will or will not explain, where it contradicts our other beliefs, and where it opens up new possibilities. (Barnes 2008: 4)

Indeed, the type of talk Barnes describes as useful in gaining understanding is not the more formalized exchange between learner and teacher which he (Barnes 2008: 4) calls **presentational talk**, but rather the more disjointed and hesitant patterns of speech that arise from trying to make sense of something, which Barnes names **exploratory talk**: the type of talk that is best facilitated in small group activities and where participants feel comfortable and at ease. As Barnes sees it too, this latter form of involvement is more conducive to pupils exploring new ideas rather than simply the transmission of those ideas from teacher to learner. It also has the added advantages of (a) giving pupils the opportunity to learn how to participate and gain an understanding of the meaning which informs that participation, as well as (b) giving them the chance to step inside an adult view of the world in order to use it for thinking and acting. In happening there would be abundant opportunities for exploratory talk between learners, and also between learners and the teacher. In addition, there would be opportunities for presentational talk at those times when ideas are summarized or presented to the group as a whole.

In addition to this, according to Barnes (2008: 11), in those group activities where exploratory talk is encouraged or other exploratory activities are undertaken, there is a real possibility for pupils to become involved in **"action knowledge"** as opposed to only **"school knowledge"**; the former being something that is integrated into the pupil's own world and has "the capacity to affect how he or she thinks, feels and acts, in school or elsewhere". The possibilities for such group activities in the production of a happening would make it a useful vehicle for gaining such action knowledge.

Although these ideas of communication and talking have been placed within the sphere of early education, it is fair to say that Barnes (2008: 6) himself does not restrict his ideas to one particular age group: he talks about working with adolescents and adults, as well as the abilities of young children. It would be unfair, too, to compartmentalize the other ideas given here: the multiple intelligences of Gardner and Krauze-Sikorska's concerns with creativity, and state that they are only applicable to younger learners. Gardner's (2012: 5) theory is applied to all cycles of education, while Krauze-Sikorska's research into creativity in school, its benefits and the problems it faces, finds echoes in theorizing concerning lower secondary level (*gimnazjum*) in Polish schools (Ziołowicz 2006: 317–332). Suffice to say, these ideas connect with descriptions given for happening in early education but should, in no way, be tied solely to that area.

4.4. A form of happening in secondary education – performance art pedagogy

In the context of secondary and higher art education in America, performance art pedagogy has been developed and used by the educationalist and artist Charles R. Garoian. Based within the teaching of art, Garoian (1999: 202) says of his pedagogy: "I was after […] a classroom experience where ideas and images, historical and contemporary, private and public could be openly problematized, interrogated, and expressed without the threat of absolute, universal, or reductive limitations". With a pedigree that includes the modernist and aesthetic concerns of happening, and the more politically and socially orientated projects of feminism and other marginalized voices in society, performance art pedagogy utilizes and explores a wealth of ideas, including ethnicity, sexual orientation, gender, race and class distinctions (Garoian 1999: 41–42). It also does this in a spirit of partnership rather than positional hierarchies. Writing as a teacher with many years of experience, Garoian (1999: 198) states:

> I believed then, as I do now, that my students had as much to contribute to the learning process as I did. […] I proposed the idea of conducting the class as a collaboration. […] Together, we would create a classroom environment where we could learn from each other, a place where we could explore and debate ideas.

Therefore, as well as having a critical-thinking dimension in relation to society, which Garoian (1999: 19) describes as "the desire to experience, question, and respond to contemporary culture and create culture anew",[57] there is also the idea of cooperation between teacher and pupils, working together to construct knowledge. To accommodate these creative disruptions, as Garoian names them, he has developed a curriculum plan where both the historical codes of art and culture can be taught while also allowing students to challenge them. As a result, his art teaching would not just

> amount to a perfunctory exercise that would, once again [as with other school subjects – MB], inscribe their [the learners – MB] bodies with socially and historically determined ideas, images, and metaphors. I did not want my pedagogy to preclude their cultural production. It was incumbent upon me to construct an art curriculum that would enable my students to learn and critique preexisting metaphors, myths, and utopias and to create new ones relevant to their lives. (Garoian 1999: 199)

Over time this curriculum itself has changed due to the involvement of the pupils. Evolving from a linear, structuralist model to one which Garoian views as being closer to a post-structuralist system, as it has increasingly accommodated the subjective positions of his pupils. As Garoian (1999: 203) states "My students found agency as they disrupted and displaced the centrality of my curriculum sequence with […] *student webs*; a multicentric system that allowed them to work both independently and collaboratively".

In this light, and referring to the educational models outlined by Bogusława D. Gołębniak (2007: 115–117), it can be seen that performance art pedagogy

---

57 The engagement for performance art which Garoian describes seems redolent with possibilities for the child in Piaget's formal operational stage.

belongs to an emancipatory-reflexive model of schooling rather than more traditional types. Taking on board its encouragement of partnership, its willingness to explore issues relating to the contemporary world and use of pupils' own experiences in a creative way in relation to culture, performance art pedagogy would also appear to fulfil some of the curriculum demands for Polish schools (Marciniak 2013: 21): the ability to work in groups, the call for learners to further their understanding of areas that are of interest to them, as well as their need to be creative and involved in culture. In addition to this, with its critical dimension in relation to society, Garoian's "desire to experience, question, and respond to contemporary culture and create culture anew", performance art pedagogy is a particularly relevant and motivating vehicle for enquiry to be used by adolescents, who are dealing with questions about themselves, the world and their place within it.[58] However, there is the question of such a critically based enterprise and one so solidly located within art education, having an application beyond that. As Garoian (1999: 202) writes, "The art classroom seemed the most sensible place for such discourse since there was nothing to lose. A marginalized discipline within the school curriculum to begin with, art was perceived as academically insignificant, a frill". This being the case, could this form of "happening" be successfully applied across other disciplines, or would it remain "marginalized", both within the arts classroom and, especially considering its emancipatory aspirations, when brought into use in the more conservative Polish schooling system? Garoian himself is aware of resistance in relation to his own teaching practice in North America, when he recounts an episode where he was called before the principal of the school in which he was working as a teacher and warned not to disrupt the order of the school:

> Why should I assume that my principal, my teaching colleagues, parents, or the student body would categorically accept any challenge that my curriculum or my students' art works would present to the status quo of the school? An effective critique engenders public discourse and critical art, and pedagogy makes such discourse possible. To continue my disruptive pedagogy, I would have to be prepared to meet any resistance with dialogue, to create a forum where a debate could ensue, to take responsibility for the public discussions that would result. (Garoian 1999: 205)

In response to what Garoian has stated for his own project within the American education system, there are a number of points to be made. First of all, his creation of a classroom environment based upon reciprocity, where everyone involved constructs the curriculum throughout the duration of the course, brings to mind

58 The *identity confusion* that adolescents experience (Erikson 1963: 261–263).

a situation in which Margaret Mead's (1970) three models of contact between the generations are enacted. Here the postfigurative imposition of a curriculum and its content gives way to a cofigurative (re)assessment of the cultural norms that are seen as "acceptable" content, to allow the inclusion of the students' own ideas and experiences which eventually make way for the prefigurative model, where the students themselves dictate the form and content of the lessons. The strength of resistance encountered to such a form of educational practice also highlights the unwillingness of the older generation of the postfigurative model, to give up its position easily. And indeed, Barbara Fatyga writes about this form of resistance, coming from this particular quarter, in relation to the Polish educational system. For Fatyga, however, the surprise, or rather sadness of such a situation, is not that there is resistance, but that the older generation does not want to enter into dialogue with the younger generation at all, either because it does not know how to, or simply, it does not want to. Summing up the results of research carried out between 1999 and 2000, Fatyga (2001: 115, translation – MB) writes: "Overall, [...] young people do not want to resign from dialogue. On the contrary, they see it as a responsibility which the older generation either do not know how to and/or do not want to take on".

Another point to be made relates to the marginalization Garoian mentions for arts subjects within the curriculum as a whole. This, however, and rather sadly, is not solely a North American phenomenon, because, as Ewa Szatan has highlighted, for more than a decade the situation for arts based subjects in Polish schools has not fared much better. In her own findings related to music provision in schools, as well as in those of other researchers writing about a range of arts subjects, the trend appears to be a worsening one. And, as Szatan and Dorota Bronk (2006: 7, translation – MB) have commented, school *should* be able to provide an environment that supports the creative process as it

> has all the right conditions: localization, well-equipped classrooms or workshops, libraries and computer labs. It also has stimulating and creative teachers who, at one and the same time, take pains to create a good atmosphere and a climate of healthy rivalry between learners – unfortunately, this very desirable vision of school, as the research shows, is far removed from Polish reality.

The reasons for the difference between *what might be* and *what is*, however, exemplifies the ways in which arts subjects are marginalized in the Polish school system on a number of different levels: the position the arts are given in the curriculum, as simply an adjunct to other subjects (Szuścik 2007: 56), the provision of training for trainee teachers (Szatan 2007: 1–15) and the barriers that arise from the model of teaching adopted or socialization practiced in schools, which hinder or block the existence of a full spectrum of creativity (see section 4.2.2 above).

Overall, Szatan and Bronk, as well as the other commentators here, could well be talking about the state of Polish compulsory education generally, although their concerns are chiefly within early education. This does not mean to say, however, that the same or similar concerns are not being voiced at secondary level. With regard to teacher training, for example, Henryka Kwiatkowska sees one of the major problems at secondary level as not only the inadequacy in training but also the fact that the true nature of what teaching involves is either not really discussed or distorted. This leads to a situation in which the complexities of teaching are hidden behind idealized notions of the teacher's work (Kwiatkowska 2006: 58–60). As an antidote to this, therefore, Kwiatkowska (2006: 60) proposes the application of Witkowski's idea of **ambivalence** across a range of teacher involvement: their relation to the profession, school as an institution, as well as (and perhaps most importantly) their relations with learners. As a result of this, and in accordance with Krzysztof Rubacha's (2007b: 61) reading of this ambivalence, the idealized world of certainty and separateness, where everything has definite meaning, is replaced by a world of uncertainty and shared experience, where there are multiple meanings. Acceptance of this latter world, meanwhile, places educational practice as a project that adheres to a sociological model for contemporary culture, which allows for diagnosis rather than idealization. In this way too, the greater breadth of teacher involvement can be explored: the fact that both the "accepted" and the "provocative" teacher from Rutkowiak's outsider as catalyst (Chapter 3, section 3.2.2) may be rejected by learners, that teachers who are too caring may hinder learner growth; while too much emphasis on discipline brings schematization and, therefore, a block to creativity. In a very real sense, meanwhile, Garoian's performance art pedagogy and happening accommodate this ambivalent model within their practice because meanings are seen to be multiple and open to interpretation, there is uncertainty both on the side of the teacher as well as the learners and there is a shared exploration of content and form.

4.5. Concluding remarks

Overall, it is possible to find counterparts in educational discourses presently known to Polish schooling for a number of the characteristics of happening outlined in Chapter 2. For instance, the need to connect happening's various elements, making sense of the whole for oneself, would, in educational terms, situate it within a constructivist paradigm. Meanwhile, its freedom from limitations in relation to form, materials, time and space, as well as the chances happening offers for exploration, would place it as a creative educational process, as would the opportunities it gives for people to meet and share ideas. However, even though these correlations exist, which should make the acceptance of a happening based practice within education possible, I have raised doubts as to whether or not this would be the case. This is because of the way the system itself accommodates, or rather as we have seen above, fails (refuses) to accommodate these already known models. In such cases, where adherence to a more traditional educational practice prevails or the socialization engaged in by the school does not permit, happening may have a problem in finding its place in education, not so much in theory, but in terms of practice.

Following on from the connections between happening and education made in this chapter and Chapter 3, in Chapter 5 a research strategy for inquiring into happening in education is outlined.

5. A research strategy for happening in education

In the previous chapters happening was viewed from various perspectives, taking into account a number of theoretical considerations. In this chapter, a research strategy is outlined which was developed and then implemented as part of an empirical study that took place in a Polish school between 2012 and 2013. The research project involved the negotiation of a number of factors towards the construction of a strategy for happening in a school setting. These included the choice of an appropriate paradigm, strategy and research techniques. It also meant finding a school that was willing to cooperate in the implementation of the project. All of these are discussed here. In addition to this, the chapter ends with a brief outline of a pilot study carried out in a non-educational setting and a main study which was undertaken in an educational environment.[59]

5.1. The aim of the research into happening

As described in Chapter 1, the present-day world is fragmented and changing, where traditional authorities and certainties no longer pertain and where it is difficult to establish one's identity as well as one's place within society as a whole. Moreover, there is a perceived need for education to help people prepare to live successfully in this world. As a way of achieving this aim, it is felt that as well as providing knowledge, school should help learners deepen their understanding of areas that are of particular interest to them while also promoting cognitive interest and creativity, including lateral thinking and transversal skills. It is also believed that pupils should develop the ability to take the initiative as well as to work individually and in groups. In relation to this, I propose happening as an appropriate practice for education to adopt.

Meanwhile, in the inquiry undertaken, there is an awareness that there are already forms of happening being used in education. These include one practised in America with secondary school learners and another in Poland with pre-school children. However, there are problems with these existing models. The former, performance art pedagogy (see Chapter 4, section 4.4), is located within one subject area (art) and in an emancipatory tradition that may make it

59 Fuller descriptions and analyses of the pilot and main study, as well as research findings, are given in Blaszk (2017).

difficult for it to be accepted by other subject areas and by a conservative educational system. The latter (see Chapter 4, section 4.3) is located in early education where, I suggest, it is either not fulfilling all of its potential or, as in the case of the happenings carried out in preschool, needs more research (Królica 2006: 100). In addition to this, and as Królica (2006: 100) comments, this research needs to be carried out at the level of happening, that is happening based in arts practice as well as school. And indeed, this would appear to fit well with the practice of happening itself, which promotes different forms of participation, as well as having educational aspirations (see Chapter 1, section 1.5).

This need, therefore, as perceived by Królica, formed the spur to a line of inquiry in which **two main questions** were formulated:

(1) How are participants involved in happening?
(2) How is this involvement situated in relation to prevailing discourses within education?

Moreover, and in relation to the research as a whole, in spite of anecdotal evidence concerning participation in happening and its educational aspirations, there has been very little empirical research carried out in relation to happening that looks at these questions specifically. Both Królica and Garoian comment upon and utilize the potentials of happening and performance in formal educational settings, but, as far as I can determine, there have been no studies carried out in these settings where learners and teachers have been actively involved in preparing and planning a happening together, and where data arising from such an occurrence has been analysed: this, therefore, formed part of my inquiry into happening in education. It also led to **a third question**:

(3) What form does the preparation and planning for a happening being created in an educational setting take?

In addition to this, it was envisaged that a variety of activities would be used during the planning and preparation of the happenings, while the process as a whole would take place within a particular subject area or areas. This meant that **a fourth question** was formulated:

(4) What types of activities would best facilitate the preparation and planning of a happening AND how would these activities support the exploration of a subject area?

Importantly too, these questions supported the reconstructive purpose of the research to be carried out which was to open up and better understand the phenomenon under analysis rather than the verification of a particular hypothesis.

5.2. The choice of research strategy

As Louis Cohen and Lawrence Manion (1996: 6) state, citing Gibson Burrell and Gareth Morgan (1979), one's conception of reality affects one's way of interpreting it, which in turn determines the assumptions one brings to the social sciences, and finally the research method one adopts. In relation to this, Burrell and Morgan present a scheme that places the social sciences either in the sphere of the natural sciences, where it is concerned with "discovering natural and universal laws regulating and determining individual and social behaviour" (Cohen and Manion 1996: 5), or a contending view, which emphasizes the uniqueness and individuality of people in relation to each other, as well as their difference in a fundamental way from inanimate natural phenomena (Cohen and Manion 1996: 5). These two viewpoints are labelled objectivist and subjectivist. The former, according to Burrell and Morgan's scheme, prefers an ontology that is realist, an epistemology that is positivist, an understanding of human nature as being determined, and a methodology that is nomothetic. In contrast, the subjectivist approach adopts a nominalist ontology, an anti-positivist epistemology and believes human nature to be voluntarist, while choosing a methodology that is idiographic. Of these assumptions, the ones relating to epistemology are for Burrell and Morgan (Cohen and Manion 1996: 6) of the upmost importance, as they "determine extreme positions on the issues of whether knowledge is something which can be acquired […] or as something which has to be personally experienced". In addition to this, and in relation to my own search for an appropriate research method, "How one aligns oneself in this particular debate profoundly affects how one will go about uncovering knowledge of social behaviour" (Cohen and Manion 1996: 6). This alignment also determines, to a large extent, the particular methodological approach one adopts, either quantitative or qualitative, or both. In relation to this debate I place myself firmly in the subjectivist paradigm.

Apart from this personal positioning when it comes to the choice of research strategy, the nature of happening is also a deciding factor. How is it possible to understand happening in relation to education while staying true to its various and complex nature? Indeed, to gain an understanding of happening, it would be a fundamental contradiction of *what it is* and *how it operates* to reduce it down to one particular aspect. The choice of a suitable research strategy is, therefore, of vital importance if as full a picture as possible of happening in an educational setting is to be gained. In connection with this, the route taken before deciding upon **bricolage** is informative. Consequently, in order to reveal some of my concerns in choosing a strategy, a brief outline will be given of a number of reasons for considering then rejecting both **ethnodrama** and **action research**. A description of bricolage as a research strategy will then be given.

5.2.1. Ethnodrama[60]

Ethnodrama is a qualitative research method which involves the construction of consensual scripts and performance scenarios related to themes important to understanding a particular experience, area or issue. These scripts and scenarios are created by informants (interested parties) who have influence over the text and representations made. Meanwhile, the research is performed by actors and is open to continual processes of validation through audience comment and debate facilitated by structured feedback to those people involved in the performance (production team and cast). In the past this has been done through the use of fax, telephone, questionnaire and interview, but at the present time it is just as likely to include e-mail, twitter and blog.

Ethnodrama was seen as an attractive prospect for researching participant involvement in happening for a number of reasons. First of all, through the use of various informant groups in the creation and recreation of scripts and scenarios, there is a space for multiple voices in the research project rather than mediation solely through one author and from an academic point of view (Mienczakowski 2008: 471). Additionally, validation and feedback through the use of readily available technologies was seen to be advantageous, as it would provide data through forms of communication readily used and acceptable to participants. Moreover, similar to happening, ethnodrama is performative with an emphasis on participation, as a result of which, because of this shared provenance, the data collected would create a truer picture of happening in education.

With regard to a procedure for ethnodrama (Mienczakowski 2008: 468–476), the following strategy was proposed in relation to happening in education. There would be an initial cycle to create a happening, this would then be enacted, during which the participants and other interested parties (teachers, learners, the happening facilitator) would create a "script" relating to / based upon their experience of what occurred. This script would then be performed with validation taking place to inform script changes before further performances and further opportunities for validation.

Enthusiasm for such an approach was counterbalanced, however, by the logistical demands of ethnodrama. It needs a rehearsal-performance space over

60 For fuller considerations of ethnodrama see Mienczakowski (2008: 468–476) and Blaszk (2009: 82–91).

a sustained period of time, and, while a school might be able to provide this, it was felt to be at odds with the practice of producing and participating in happenings which are briefer, more guerrilla type activities, and where there is limited or no rehearsal (Kirby 1966: 48–49). Included in this, too, was the procedure suggested for ethnodrama transposed onto happening: participants and informants would be involved in a happening the ideas from which would then form the basis for a script to be performed by actors, and which would then be validated for further performances and further validation. This was felt to be too cumbersome a mechanism for what happening can be, and particularly the form of happening I was interested in researching. In addition to this, in the performance of ethnodrama actors are used, which is generally not the case with happening (see Chapter 2, section 2.1.1.2), while in my own experience as a happener participants are from various walks of life (not trained actors as with ethnodrama) and involved for a limited period of time. The brevity of happening, therefore, seemed to be in danger, while, most importantly, I felt the true aims of the research might be lost to the needs of "putting on a show".

5.2.2. Action research

Another method I considered was action research. Although often placed within a qualitative paradigm, there are researchers who believe it lies uneasily there, favouring instead to describe it as praxis (O'Brien 2001): acting upon the conditions one finds oneself in order to change them. This emancipatory idea of praxis provided an important reason for wanting to use action research because, as a happener, I was interested in how answers to the research questions might affect my continuing practice. Another reason for wanting to choose action research was its perceived similarity to happening and its flexibility. The proposed action research model was to be based upon a simple cyclical scheme put forward by Stephen Kemmis which includes four steps:

- plan,
- action,
- observe,
- reflect (O'Brien 2001: 1).

These steps more or less replicate the ones that occur when I prepare and carry out a happening[61] so that I felt the research project would not overly interfere with the

61 Steps similar to these have occurred on a more casual basis in the planning, preparation and enactment of happenings with which I have been involved. Because of this,

happening process, but rather accommodate it. Additionally, the modular-cyclical format proposed by Kemmis allowed for flexibility in the number of cycles to be used within the research project: from one to many. As a result, I felt it would offer the brevity more appropriate to happening, unlike ethnodrama. Meanwhile, through adaptations to Kemmis' four step cycle, I proposed making the research procedure "fit" the usual procedure for a happening, as carried out by myself and fellow happeners. Part of this would be the videotaping of the happening at the action step, which, in effect, was also to double up as the observation step. I also perceived the reflection step to be part of an already existing happening procedure, which usually takes the shape of an informal, post-happening discussion among participants. Therefore, the three proposed methods of data collection / interpretation included:

- videotaping of the happening taking place (to be interpreted by the researcher),
- first discussion of the happening between its participants (including the researcher),
- second discussion of the happening, after viewing the video (with the possibility of rewinding and fast-forwarding the video during discussion).

This second discussion would provide a means of verification of the research data through what was essentially triangulation.

A strict adoption of this method was eventually rejected, however, as I felt it placed me too much as a researcher inquiring into a particular phenomenon, rather than **someone who would *also* be involved with other people, engaged in activities and events as much as they would be**. In this case, an action research method which emphasized the participatory nature of my inquiry appeared to be a better choice (see below, section 5.2.3). I also felt that by using action research outright, as described in the Kemmis model, there would be a danger of concentrating on a secondary concern of the research, relating to development of my own practice of happening, rather than the primary concern, which is about generating knowledge about involvement in happening and how it relates to educational discourse. In addition to this, the element of triangulation is reductive, whereas an important impetus for the research project was that it would generate knowledge about happening in relation to involvement and education.

I believe an equivalence can be found. There is, for instance, a planning stage where ideas are brought together by the happeners involved (plan). Then the happening is enacted (action), at which time the happeners are observers of one another and what is occurring (observe). What occurs during the happening is then usually discussed after the happening, with ideas and suggestions feeding into further happenings (reflect).

5.2.3. Bricolage as a research strategy

As outlined in Chapter 2, happening exists under various names and is difficult to classify because of its complex and contradictory nature. As a result, it needs a research strategy that will allow for its multiform and changing character, a strategy that will not attempt to classify but open up understanding and, from my own position as a practitioner (happener-teacher), help in the development of happening in education. Bricolage was chosen as a research strategy because it was felt to be "sympathetic" to happening in these ways.

The French word *bricoleur* is used to denote a handyperson who uses the tools at hand to carry out the work she/he is doing at any one particular time. In relation to the social sciences it was first used by Claude Lévi-Strauss (Sadon-Osowiecka 2009a: 75) to describe the way in which language and myth are constructed by (primitive) societies; especially the way in which anticipation is used to categorize phenomena as they are assimilated into their existing systems of knowledge. In this way also, Lévi-Strauss was able to show that the same facts observed by different researchers would be interpreted in different ways. Staying within the social sciences but bringing the use of the term up-to-date, Joe L. Kincheloe (2010: 7) states that "In the first decade of the twenty-first century bricolage is typically understood to involve the process of employing […] methodological strategies as they are needed in the unfolding context of the research situation". Further to this, together with McLaren (Kinchloe and McLaren 2005: 311), he writes that its

> deep interdisciplinarity seeks to modify the disciplines and the view of research brought to the negotiating table constructed by the bricolage […]. Everyone leaves the table informed by the dialogue in a way that idiosyncratically influences the research methods they subsequently employ. The point of the interaction is not standardized agreement as to some reductionist notion of the "proper interdisciplinary research method" but awareness of the diverse tools in the researcher's toolbox. The form such deep interdisciplinarity may take is shaped by the object of inquiry in question.

It is clear from this extract that for its authors the interdisciplinary nature of bricolage makes it a dynamic research strategy that is, above all, responsive to the subject of its research. It is also clear that they view it as developmental for the researcher who chooses to use it. These characteristics along with its antireductionist stance, place it, therefore, in a qualitative research tradition (Sadon-Osowiecka 2009b: 103–140) which is "built upon the philosophical bases of phenomenology, hermeneutics and symbolic-interactionism" (Pilch and Bauman 2001: 270, translation – MB). Its transformative possibilities, both for the research strategy and the researcher, also place it within a critical, emancipatory tradition (Kinchloe and McLaren 2005: 307). As part of this particular bricolage strategy, in terms of responsiveness to research subject, the inquiry can also be located as action research within a participatory inquiry paradigm (Guba and Lincoln 2005: 195) where epistemologically, experiential knowing is seen to be of prime importance and that this "arises through participation with others" (Reason 1994: 333). In addition, in terms of axiology, there is no one fixed truth, but rather a shared search for perspectives that are relevant to the participants in their continuing development (Reason 1994: 334). The emancipatory nature of this involvement in knowledge being evident in that it involves critical subjectivity and voice, where the "primary voice is manifest through aware self-reflective action, secondary voices in illuminating theory [...] and other presentational forms" (Heron and Reason 1997: 290).[62] This emancipatory character of participatory inquiry is also, I believe, close to that of happening; where the participants in both are empowered to act with the possibility of changing the conditions in which they find themselves.

Summing up, bricolage would appear to be the most suitable research strategy for an inquiry into happening based in education; its multidisciplinary character corresponds to happening, allowing for its multiform and changing character, enabling analysis of its complex and contradictory nature. Moreover, as a research strategy it also accommodates the participatory nature of the inquiry.

5.3. Research methods and techniques

Having touched upon the characteristics of bricolage, its application as a research strategy will now be considered. In doing so, a procedure outlined by Kincheloe is described as well as a variation of the rhizome structure of Felix Guattari and Gilles Deleuze, which provided a model for the procedure's implementation. This is followed by descriptions of the research techniques employed and a pilot happening which was carried out in a non educational setting.

5.3.1. A procedure called POET

A procedure Kincheloe (2010: 33–40) outlines for using the bricolage is to take a POET (point of entry text) and thread it through a variety of conceptual maps.[63] The POET for my inquiry into happening in education consisted of the research questions presented at the beginning of this chapter (section 5.1) and research

62 See also Guba and Lincoln's (2005: 191–216) consideration of the particpatory inquiry paradigm.

63 Kincheloe (2010: 33–34) gives a number of conceptual maps for a hypothetical research question based within ethnic studies: the ways in which contemporary racism in America is different from racism in the past.

data gained from the enactment of two happenings in an educational setting, including their planning and preparation. The questions and the data were then threaded through conceptual maps arising from this theoretical study. These included the following:

- **discourses of social theory** – constructivism, critical theory, structuralism, poststructuralism;
- **research genres and methodologies** – qualitative analysis, ethnography;
- **disciplinary / interdisciplinary departmentalizations of knowledge** – art, education / pedagogy, performance, philosophy, psychology, sociology, anthropology, political science;
- **performance domains** – happening, theatre;
- **pedagogical domains** – progressivism, early education, creative education, pedagogy of drama, pedagogy of happening, performance art pedagogy.

Additionally, the material analysed throughout the research project originated from different areas:

- **knowledge sources** – artefacts, oral, print, photographs, video, internet, visuals, books, journals.

Kincheloe describes the benefits of the use of many and different conceptual maps in two ways. Firstly, they offer multiple perspectives and thereby new forms of knowledge production, setting up "the possibility for discerning relationships and processes that open up new conceptual vistas [...] [so that] conditions are created for analytical and interpretive spontaneity, random associations that yield profound insights, and novelty" (Kinchloe 2010: 34). Following on from this, he links this openness to multiplicity to the researcher-researched relationship where "Bricoleurs in their valuing of diverse forms of knowledge [...] come to value the abilities and insights of those who they research", thereby creating "more egalitarian relationships with [the] individuals being researched" (Kinchloe 2010: 6). There is also, however, a note of caution, as all this "demands a new level of research self-consciousness and awareness of the numerous contexts in which any researcher is operating" (Kinchloe 2010: 7), as well as the need "to develop a comfort with ambiguity" (Kinchloe 2010: 35).

In relation to this, Teresa Sadon-Osowiecka (2009b: 135, translation – MB) gives one of the characteristics of bricolage as "a lack of a clear and final conception at the beginning as to the final result". Additionally, and importantly, Sadon-Osowiecka (2009a: 79, translation – MB) states that it is something different to triangulation "which also connects different methods and techniques" but which seeks to "present an objective or naturalistic vision of the world which is not contextualized [...] and establish beforehand the picture that will be obtained from the research results, whereas the picture of the world established from the results of the bricolage appear only at the end of the research".

In a way, bricolage's deeply interdisciplinary character, with the focus on process, is reminiscent of Guattari and Deleuze's (1987: 21) rhizome, which "connects any point to any other point, and [whose] traits are not necessarily linked to traits of the same nature; it brings into play very different regimes of signs, and even non sign states. The rhizome is reducible to neither the One or the multiple". It is also reminiscent of Deleuze (1993: 81) in considering Leibniz, where he describes the chaotic world in which we live as

> a "chaosmos" [where]...Even God desists from a Being who compares worlds and chooses the richest compossible. He becomes Process, a process that at once affirms incompossibilities and passes through them. The play of the world has changed in a unique way, because now it has become the play that diverges. Beings are pushed apart, kept open through divergent series and incompossible totalities that pull them outside, instead of being closed upon the compossible and convergent world that they express from within.[...] It is a world of captures instead of closures.

The metaphors of the rhizome and the "chaosmos" are used here by the authors to give form to ideas of connectivity, multifariousness and irreducibility, with an emphasis upon process and divergence, all of which lie at the heart of their project. However, in relation to bricolage, perhaps a more appropriate metaphor and one that seems to bring these two ideas together is the tumbleweed. This ball-shaped plant, whose volume is made up of an entanglement of organic strands, offers a model for the intertwining thread of the POET as it passes through different conceptual maps. In addition to this, the fact that the tumbleweed breaks free from its roots and is blown about by the wind provides another metaphor for the bricolage's dynamic movement whose direction is free rolling and difficult (impossible) to predict beforehand.

In order to visualize this model more clearly: rhizome-tumbleweed – POET – conceptual maps, a line which represents the POET can be drawn. This line can then be given different qualities (continuous line, dots, dashes, dash-dot-dash or dash-dot-dot-dash) to represent its passage through some of the different conceptual maps used for the inquiry into happening in school: for example, artefacts, pedagogy of creativity, constructivism, ritual in education and critical theory. The result is shown in Figure 2.

Figure 2: POET being threaded through different conceptual maps

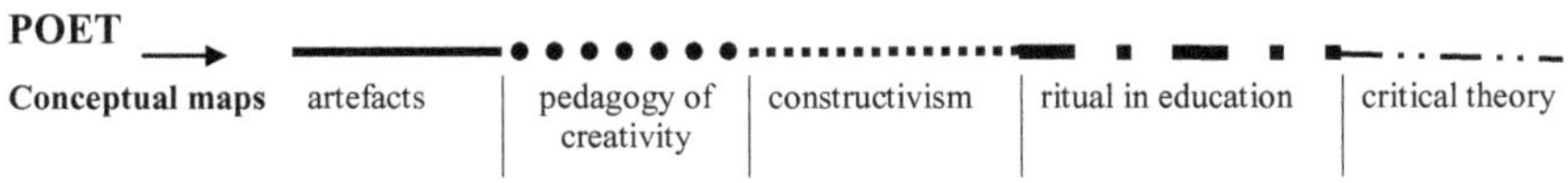

However, this provides a model based upon a linear process, whereas Kincheloe (2010: 34) is adamant that bricolage and the passage of the POET through the conceptual maps is anything but linear, its "feedback looping process" freeing it up from "step-by-step linearity". Therefore, it is necessary to transpose the line and its different qualities (the POET passing through the different conceptual maps) onto the rhizome-tumbleweed. This gives a model as shown in Figure 3 (a combination of all of the different line qualities given in Figure 2, taking up, more or less, the whole of the central part of the model shown on Figure 3).

This model shows the workings of my own POET as artefacts (the continuous black line) are analysed and can be seen to touch upon issues to do with pedagogy of creativity (the dots on the right-hand side of the model), but also intersects and crosses over itself in relation to the other conceptual maps of constructivism, ritual in education and critical theory (a combination of all the dot and dash combinations given above and here within most of the central portion of the model). At yet another point, meanwhile, issues to do with pedagogy of creativity run parallel to, or, depending on one's interpretation, are entwined with constructivism (the lower central part of the model). The truly dynamic nature of the rhizome-tumbleweed, however, is only really grasped when one considers it as a three-dimensional model, one that in its free roaming movement offers up many more and different viewpoints, all of which reveal "new" intersections, crossings, parallels and entwinings.

Figure 3: A rhizome-tumbleweed model

5.3.2. Research techniques

Bricolage is open to new combinations in response to the subject of the research. At a fundamental level, and in relation to the research project which was realized, this included the type of research methods to be employed. Taking up Geertz's (1980) ideas concerning the blurring of genres, research into happening under the umbrella of bricolage lies somewhere between **case study** and **action research** – the former, in that it focuses on particular groups of participants in a number of happenings;[64] the latter, in that as a happener-teacher involved in the practices of happening and teaching – "immersed in the phenomenon being researched" (Pilch and Bauman 2001: 308, translation – MB), it seemed inevitable that the research findings would feed back into those practices and have some form of impact upon them.

The research techniques adopted in a pilot study and the main study (Table 1) included **auto-narrative** and **retrospective auto-reflection**, as well as **autobiographical interview** and **group discussion.** The group discussions, meanwhile,

64 Case study as a method is understood in many different ways. This is explored in some detail by Marta Galewska-Kustra. Here I apply Martyn Hammersley's (Galewska-Kustra 2009: 232) definition in which the term *case study* can be applied to research that analyzes a number of cases in detail or sometimes only one.

took the form of participants **viewing and commenting upon visuals (photographs / video)** produced throughout the research project. Additionally, and in an echo of ethnodrama in relation to the types of input / feedback proposed, a **blog** was set up which acted as a point of contact between myself and the participants, as well as providing data for the inquiry. Throughout the planning and preparation of the school happenings, a variety of activities and objects were used and produced, descriptions of which also comprised part of the research data to be analysed. Finally, as classrooms and other places used also played a part in the happening research project, a **consideration of location** was also undertaken.

Table 1: Research techniques: Pilot study and main study

	Pilot study – happening in a non-education environment	**Main study – two happenings in an education environment**
Data and data gathering techniques	– Video and photographs from happening – Auto-narrative – Retrospective auto-reflection – Autobiographical interview – Group discussion viewing video of a pilot study (the happening *Polish Immigration / Polska imigracja*)	– Videos and photographs from happenings – Auto-narrative – Retrospective auto-reflection – Autobiographical interview – Group discussions looking at visuals – video (the happening *Tolerance*) and photographs (*Niggle Happening*) – Posts from a blog – Descriptions of activities / artefacts / locations

These techniques were proposed for a number of reasons. First and foremost, they were the least invasive with regard to happening and the needs of the happeners and participants. Another reason was the variety it offered in relation to personal preference. For example, the use of auto-narrative in the form of diary entries gave me a way of recording my impressions with which I was comfortable, while the autobiographical interview was used because the happeners and participants preferred to discuss their involvement. The blog also offered most participants a space in which they felt they could express themselves in writing in connection with the happenings and sessions.

The use of a small digital camera and camcorder to record events, and then viewing and commenting upon them, is a fairly ubiquitous experience nowadays. This is a position which is upheld by Mike Ball and Greg Smith (2008: 303) who see the main form of pictorial representation in postmodern society as electronic and the reading position adopted as that of the **interactive user**. This is especially true when one considers the target group of the main study (see below 5.4). Additionally, the use of the camcorder to record happenings is readily accepted or may be an integral part of the enactment. In this situation, therefore, the concepts of **video active context** and **fluid wall**, from Wesley Shrum, Ricardo Duque and Timothy Brown (2005: 10) readily apply, where "No invisible wall separates actors from production crew in the video active context. Rather, a *fluid wall* separates participants who discuss filming, frame shots – and may exchange roles". This is because, as they comment further, "Not only is the illusion of non-presence unimportant for most purposes, the maintenance of an invisible wall results in loss of opportunities" (Shrum, Duque and Brown 2005: 10).

5.3.2.1. A pilot study

In addition to the above, the happening *Polish Immigration / Polska imigracja* was enacted in February 2010 and provided information useful for the planning and coordination of happening in a school environment. In this, it acted as a pilot study, "a check on the research tools and research project as a whole" (Pilch and Bauman 2001: 260, translation – MB), as well as ensuring "the optimal use" (p. 262) of the tools to be used. Equally importantly, pilot studies also "give [...] a picture of the main features of the environment to be researched" (p. 260), which, in the case of the happening project, allowed me to view that environment from another perspective: as a researcher and not simply a happener.

Indeed, as a pilot study, *Polish Immigration...* let me trial the procedure for carrying out interviews that formed part of the data collection for the main study. This meant asking respondents to talk about their involvement in the pilot happening in terms of what occurred **before**, **during** and **after** the enactment of the happening, which, in turn, gave them scope to talk about the **preparation** and **planning** that took place, **events that occurred during the happening**, and **anything that took place afterwards** they felt was **linked to the happening itself**, or their **reflections** since enacting the happening. Another important technique taken from the pilot happening was the integral use of photography and video in its enactment: for documentation of the happening and to make a film, but also as a means of data collection. This confirmed the use of a similar strategy in the main study. Additionally, data from the pilot happening confirmed the fact that if happening was to be analysed in education, it could not simply be viewed as an isolated event – an enactment without preparation and planning. This was because throughout the pilot study the process of creating the happening, although not always explicit as a particular procedure, was nonetheless vital to what occurred on the day it took place. This was especially evident in the interview responses recounting events leading up to the enactment of *Polish Immigration…*, as well as my own accounts of what took place up to the enactment. In this situation, therefore, it appeared appropriate that analysis of the preparation and planning accompanying a happening should play a central role and have to be included in any research project that was to look at happening in education. Table 2 (section 5.4 below) shows the form of involvement in the pilot study during the planning, preparation and enactment of the happening.

5.4. The form, place and duration of the main study

The main study was longer in duration and more complex than the pilot, it also involved more people. Originally, it was envisaged that the study would take place over one semester in either a primary (*szkoła podstawowa*), lower-secondary (*gimnazjum*) or upper-secondary (*liceum*) school. It was also envisaged that when a school at one of these levels had agreed to cooperate, two classes with different teachers would be involved, to give a broad range of data and to allow similarities and differences in practice to be noticed. The intention was to work with learners and teachers in the preparation, planning and enactment of two happenings – one happening to be enacted by each class. Additionally, details relating to the theme, place and form of the happening, including preparation and planning, were to be decided between myself, the teachers and the learners. Initially, too, because of my profile: artist, English teacher and native English speaker, I wanted to work with teachers and learners that had a humanities profile and good command of the English language or, simply, English language classes that would be interested in co-operating on a project to create a happening. With this basic outline of my intentions, teachers were approached directly. This included those I met in the Tri-City conglomerate (Gdańsk, Sopot and Gdynia), in my role as supervisor of teaching practices for student teachers in the English Department of the University of Gdańsk. It also comprised those teachers I met at a conference for language teachers from the Tri-City area, which took place in the late autumn of 2011.

There was a problem setting up a research project in the form outlined above, however. Many of the teachers approached were enthusiastic about the opportunity to work cooperatively to produce a happening, although when it came to setting up the project in school, there was reticence: in one case, because the school director found it "too risky", which appears to confirm the problems for creativity within compulsory schooling (see Chapter 4, section 4.2.2).

Because of the problems encountered, the research project finally negotiated took place in a Gdańsk *liceum* and was in the form of extra-curricular sessions linked to the teaching of English as a foreign language. From mid-November 2012 until the end of June 2013, excluding school breaks, I met the participants involved in the project once a week for ninety minutes. In total, there were twenty-four sessions, resulting in two happenings. The sessions and the happenings were carried out during the two school terms: 12 sessions and one happening in the winter term and 12 sessions and one happening in the summer term. Each of these cycles consisted of preparation and planning leading to the enactment of happenings, and then interviews, where the sessions and the happenings were discussed. Throughout both cycles there were 7 people involved: myself and 6 learners from the *liceum*. The learners, between 15 and 16 years of age, were all in the first grade of the *liceum*, in various classes. There were 5 female learners and one male.

The first school happening, *Tolerance*, took the form of street interviews where the participants worked in pairs and asked passers-by about their views on tolerance. It was carried out on Saturday, 26 January 2013, in the Old Town of Gdańsk. The second school happening, *Niggle Happening*, involved participants writing their dislikes ("niggles") on a cleaning cloth and then using it to clean their homes, after which they sat and reflected on the experience whilst taking refreshments. Each participant performed their own individual version of the happening working together with someone who documented it. The happenings took place between the 8th and 17th of June 2013. Table 2 below shows the forms of involvement in the happenings of the main study, as well as their planning and preparation.

Table 2: The form, place and duration of the research project

	Pilot study – happening in a non-education environment		**Main study – two happenings in an education environment**		
Title	Happening #1: *Polish Immigration / Polska imigracja*	Planning and preparation of happening #1	Happening #2: *Tolerance*	Happening #3: *Niggle Happening*	Planning and preparation of happening # 2, 3
Form of involvement	– Group of artists / happeners – (3 people) – Approx. 2 hours on a main street in Newcastle, England	– Informal contact – Group of happeners incl. myself (3 people) – Contact and time not noted	– Group of participants, myself and a happener as observers (8 people) – Approx. 2 hours on a main street in Gdańsk	– Group of participants and myself (6 people) – Unspecified length of time in individual participants' homes	– Sessions (part of happening project in English) – Group of participants and myself (7 people) – 24 sessions over two semesters in a Gdańsk *liceum* – 48 teaching hours[65]
Research strategy	Bricolage (pilot study / data for main study)		Bricolage (main study)		

65 One teaching hour is equivalent to 45 minutes.

5.5. Concluding remarks

My preferred research strategy for inquiring into happening in an educational setting was bricolage. This is because it allows for multiple viewpoints and a generation of knowledge rather than the confirmation of a particular hypothesis or theory – which was not the aim of the inquiry. The use of bricolage also means a variety of research techniques can be used so that the needs and preferences of the people involved in the inquiry can be served. The possibility for such variety was also in keeping with the demands of the research. These were complex in that it was participatory and involved inquiring into happening, a practice that can take a variety of forms. The choice of only one technique, therefore, ran the risk of being limiting rather than generative. In connection with this, the alignment of one particular form of bricolage, Kinchloe's POET model, with a version of Deleuze and Guattari's rhizome – rhizome-tumbleweed – meant that not only the element of participation and complexity of happening could be catered for but also the dynamic nature of the research itself, which comprised of a number of different people and locations, and took place over a sustained period of time.

In the conclusion, concerns recounted in this and the previous chapters are brought together to show how schooling in its present form in Poland is failing in its stated aims and how the use of happening could actually help achieve them. Additionally, a number of problems that might be encountered in the implementation of happening in school are discussed as well as those related to the setting up of the research project itself.

Conclusion

At both national (Marciniak 2013) and international level (Delors et al 1996, *European Union Key Competences for Education* 2009, Narayan 2012), there is a perceived need for education to prepare people to live successfully in the world as it exists today. This world is viewed as unstable and ever-changing (Beck 2002, Szkudlarek and Śliwerski 1991), where it is difficult for people to forge and then sustain one particular identity (Bauman 1993, 2011, Witkowski 2007). Education should, therefore, facilitate the development of skills that will give people the ability (flexibility) to live in such a world. At the international level these skills include lateral thinking and transversal skills, as well as adaptability (*European Union Key Competences for Education* 2009), while at a national level, relating particularly to compulsory schooling in Poland, they are seen to be the development of cognitive interest and involvement in culture, the ability to take the initiative and work in groups (Marciniak 2013: 21). Meanwhile, at both a national and international level, the development of creativity is seen to be of vital importance.

In relation to this situation, however, compulsory education, especially in Poland, is seen to be wanting. For, whereas Marciniak proposes a curriculum which would allow learners to pursue their interests (Marciniak 2013: 15), develop critical awareness (p. 19) and make decisions relating to their own learning (p. 22), when it comes to the education in which they are involved, the situation is very different. For instance, in her summation of Polish schooling as a whole, Klus-Stańska (2002: 79–83) sees it as extremely conservative (a form which Gołębniak (2007: 109) would classify as traditional), where learners have to accept knowledge given to them by a teacher or through a textbook, which, in fact, may not be of interest to them. Furthermore, there is little or no encouragement for pupils to search for knowledge on their own behalf or have an opinion about it, as school determines what is worthy of study and how it should be studied. Indeed, more creative involvement, in the form of research or critical involvement, is discouraged as being disruptive (Klus-Stańska 2006: 65–68), because as far as this more traditional form of schooling is concerned, the learner's "job" is to accumulate ready-made knowledge and then give it back through testing, without necessarily having ever experienced it. Therefore, with regard to Marciniak's intentions that skills appropriate to achieving success in the contemporary world be promoted, there still appears to be an (over)emphasis on what he terms a "solid foundation of general knowledge" (Marciniak 2013: 9, translation – MB), the very area that the *European Key*

Competences play down in favour of skills more conducive to functioning in the modern world.

In connection with the above, in contrast to traditional schooling, happening in education would appear to offer the possibility of active engagement, both in finding and linking ideas together (*chance* and *dream logic*), as well as the interpretation of those ideas. With the onus for choice and interpretation placed upon the participants involved, there is also critical engagement, while this choice is open to all participants (*multicentrism*) and covers a range of different areas (*dissolution of borders between forms*). Additionally, with the latter there is no form that dominates nor any one participant voice (*indeterminancy*). This means that whereas traditional schooling emphasizes the cognitive to the negation of the bodily and physical, happening allows these as legitimate ways of knowing about the world. It also means that the teacher is not the only and most important source of knowledge.

There are also other consequences for schooling linked to the use of happening. The possibility for physical involvement changes the dynamic of the place of school to one in which, instead of sitting at desks facing forwards, accepting the knowledge given by the teacher, participants can be engaged in different groupings in different areas of the classroom, or beyond it, finding out things for themselves. This changes the role of the pupil to one of an active participant, where there is a possibility for exploration which facilitates the development of cognitive abilities and not just the presentation of already thought out ideas (Barnes 2008: 4). It also makes the teacher a partner in a process of learning rather than the purveyor of a product that she/he gives to the pupils who, in return, are expected to "patiently receive, memorize and repeat" (Freire 2000: 72). The distinction between space and place (de Certeau 1988: 117–118, Patraka 1999: 109–110) also becomes significant, as school becomes a location where the individualized and transgressive power of space can exist alongside the more formalized and institutionalized aegis of place. It is also a location in which the symbolic (antistructure) is present, where metaphor and anti-myth are to the fore, and not an indexed involvement, in which myth, metonymy and syntagma are strong (Dembiński 2005: 39–51). And again, in relation to the teacher, partnership with participants allows for a facilitative process to unfold where the subjunctive mood is prominent, a situation which connects more to the teacher as a liminal servant (McLaren 1993: 113–119) rather than a technocratic model.

The fact that happening can be of real life and inclusive of many ideas which are actively explored (enacted), means it is open to a range of issues outside of traditional school subjects, including those arising from the participants' own experiences and tackled in a way that is different to the more passive treatment adopted by school. In this it is close to Dewey's (1956, 1966) educational project. It also, in turn, leads to a situation where happening is not only engaged with the world (and the lives of the participants) but also provides a form of involvement (forum) where participants can voice their ideas about that world. In addition to this, because of its performative aspect where ideas are actively pursued, there is a possibility for an element of praxis where these ideas are put into practice. This, along with the critical aspect of happening, also means there is a possibility of implementing ideas for change – an empowerment of the individual which Szkudlarek (2009: 207–209) views as the basis for a critical pedagogy and which Melosik (2007: 311–316) links back to Dewey and the fundamental democratic nature of his educational project.

Happening enacted in a school, and therefore the possibilities outlined above, need not be restricted to one particular level of education. At lower (Królica 2006) or higher levels (Garoian 1999), it would afford forms of engagement where participants would be involved with one another, objects and ideas in ways that go beyond those usually advocated by traditional schooling. In addition to what has been mentioned above, this could include a variety of intelligences: linguistic, musical, logical-mathematical, visual-spatial, personal (interpersonal and intrapersonal) and physical (bodily-kinaesthetic) (Gardner 1999). It might also offer different ways for participants to be involved with objects and other people. With regard to the former, this may be working with objects to achieve a goal (Kruk 2008: 139), to create a product (Bolt 2004: 9), or as a "partner" (non-human) in a shared enterprise (Domańska 2009: 54). In terms of contact with other people, it could be any one of Rutkowiak's (1997: 88–98) proposals in connection with the outsider where, amongst other things, participants learn from a person with whom they have an intimate subject to subject relation, or a person who acts as a catalyst, helping the participants to develop themselves. Additionally, it might involve discussions where a consensus is reached (Matynia 2009: 80) or where there is no consensus but recognition and acceptance of different points of view (Witkowski 2000: 14–15, Kwaśnica 1995: 23–24).

As well as involvement with others, objects and ideas, there is an intrinsic creative aspect to happening that has an influence on how participants are engaged. This entails embarking on a process whose aim is not defined from the outset, but which is open to modification from new and different influences as it is pursued (Nęcka 1994: 21). This means that participants are not only cognitively but also critically involved, so that creative involvement in this instance is not working in a prescribed way but one in which the autonomy of the participant is emphasized and where they have freedom to explore and experiment. This involves close contact with others where different views and ideas are exchanged (Sajdak 2008: 58–60), but also the danger that what is done or produced may not be acceptable to society at large (Szmidt 2007: 51). Additionally, these aspects include elements such as spontaneity and flexibility, as well as synthesis, where apparently irreconcilable elements are brought together as a whole. Meanwhile, the reactions to such activity from those partaking in it may be surprise (shock) and mistrust, followed by reassessment and acceptance (Nęcka 1994: 21–22).

As mentioned above, the fact that happening might offer all of these possibilities does not mean, however, that school, especially a model which is conservatively grounded, will readily accept it. Garoian's (1999: 205) experience of trying to implement his performance art pedagogy at the secondary level in America is a case in point, where, although his teaching received the approbation of learners, it was not understood or approved of by the school authorities. Furthermore, this type of reaction in Polish school would appear all the more possible if happening were viewed as a creative process, for – as various researchers have found / commented upon – creativity in Polish schools is permissible only if it is recognized as such (music, art, drama) (Szatan 2007: 1) or follows a particular (schematized) format (ludic-fantastic, aesthetic-artistic) (Klus-Stańska 2006: 63–65). Generally, however, creativity and the full force of its potential, as mentioned above, is not always admissible; rather, learner involvement as a researcher may be tolerated, whereas on a critical level it is frowned upon as insubordination (Klus-Stańska 2006: 65–68). At the cognitive level especially, this leads to a situation where learners follow a given path rather than search for one themselves (Klus-Stańska 2002: 221–252), and where they are forced to look for the one right answer (Nowicka 2010: 265). Indeed, it can be speculated that any number of the reasons Nęcka (1999: 112–188) gives as obstacles to creativity in school exist in the Polish setting.

Taking into account what has been described, carrying out research into happening in Polish school has not been without its problems. An initial difficulty with regard to the inquiry outlined in Chapter 5, was to find a school to cooperate with. Considering what has been written in this book (Chapter 4, sections 4.4 and 4.2.2), although learners may want to be involved in happening-type lessons and the engagement they promote (Garoian 1999: 203), the school administration might not be so enthusiastic. Additionally, it is possible that Polish schooling is not actually ready for the type of creativity happening has to offer, which involves participants searching for their own path as a researcher or as a critically aware learner, rather than passively accepting what is given by a teacher, or following a prescribed line of creative inquiry.

Moreover, on the level of research strategy, the complex nature of happening means that such an inquiry should not be limited to one particular area or aspect. This was especially true for the empirical research carried out as part of this inquiry into happening,[66] as it was about generating knowledge rather than verifying a particular hypothesis about its practice. Indeed, the adopted bricolage model, which utilizes Kinchloe's (2010) POET and is informed by a version of Delueze and Guattari's (1987) rhizome – rhizome-tumbleweed – allowed for a variety of educational discourses to be considered, as well as other departmentalizations of knowledge, such as performance, philosophy, psychology, sociology, anthropology and political science. Additionally, it permitted a range of research techniques to be used, best suited to happening and responsive to the participants' preferences with regard to how they wanted to be involved in the research: diary, blog, interview, discussion, photographs and video. Moreover, the dynamic nature of the strategy meant that it was open to change during the implementation of the research. This was important as the inquiry was participatory in nature and took place over an extended period of time, which meant unforeseen reactions and events were bound to (and did) occur. Such a dynamic and rich research strategy, meanwhile, enabled these reactions and events to be taken into account, while also still allowing the main focus of the research to remain – how participants are involved in happening and how this relates to existing educational discourses. It also permitted the consideration of secondary questions relating to the preparation and planning of a happening and the types of activities to be used with respect to a particular subject area.

To finish, it seems fair to say that to help learners construct a "Self" in a world that is fragmented and unpredictable, to create their own narratives of the world, as it were, then for this to be successful, it cannot be done using a model of schooling that was (a) constructed in and relevant to another (former) time and (b) ignores the reality of the learners' lives, as well as the wider world within which they are located. It would appear vital, therefore, that the education system pays heed to the needs of all those who are involved in it. Furthermore, as was mentioned in Chapter 1 (section 1.4), in Polish educational thought there is a willingness for development and not just in the area of didactics, but also in the consideration of conditions that would allow the implementation of "new" educational models and their acceptance by society as a whole. In this case, happening would appear to be a suitable practice to adopt. Additionally, in a world where active participation of the individual is called for, both in the construction

---

66 See Blaszk (2017).

of their own world and that of the greater society to which they belong, education through the use of happening could help promote these aspirations as well as allow learners to take part in the processes necessary for their realization. Indeed, at the time of writing, in the centenary year of the publication of *Democracy and Education*, Dewey's call for the active involvement of learners in school and on from that (as a result of it) their active involvement in society as a whole, appears as pertinent as ever if society is to continue to be created anew so as to ensure its relevance to *all* who are part of it.

Gdańsk 2016

References

Ablewicz, Krystyna (1997). Język potoczny jako warunek dialogu edukacyjnego – w poszukiwaniu języka pedagogiki. *Edukacja: studia, badania, innowacja* 3 (59): 15–25.

Aleksander, Zdzisław (1992). Język potoczny jako płaszczyzna porozumienia się pokoleń. In: Joanna Rutkowiak (ed.). *Pytanie, dialog, wychowanie*. Warszawa: Wydawnictwo Naukowe PWN, 231–247.

Aleksander, Zdzisław (2009). *Szansa na międzypokoleniowy dialog w kontekście rozumienia słów w zakresie moralności*. Gdańsk: Wydawnictwo Uniwersytetu Gdańskiego.

Austin, John L. (1975). *How to Do Things with Words*. Cambridge, Massachusetts: Harvard University Press.

Ayres, Robert. *A Sky Filled with Shooting Stars: A Resident Alien Visits the Art World*. Available at <http://www.askyfilledwithshootingstars.com/wordpress/?p=1371>. Accessed 1 April 2012.

Bakhtin, Mikhail (1984). *Rabelais and His World*. Trans. Helene Iswolsky. Bloomington: Indiana University Press.

Ball, Mike and Greg Smith (2008). *Technologies of Realism? Ethnographic Uses of Photography and Film*. In: Paul Atkinson et al. (eds.). *The Handbook of Ethnography*. Los Angeles: Sage, 302–319.

Bałachowicz, Józefa (2009). Ocena nowej podstawy programowej klas I–III w świetle podmiotowego modelu edukacji. *Problemy Wczesnej Edukacji*. Special Edition: 9–17.

Baranowa, Anna, Bernadeta Stano (2006). *Linia podziału* Tadeusza Kantora – wielość interpretacji. *Dekada Literacka* 6(220): 110–125.

Barnes, Douglas (2008). Exploratory talk for learning. In: Neil Mercer, Steve Hodgkinson (eds.). *Exploring Talk in School*. Los Angeles: Sage, 1–16.

Barnes, Douglas (2010). Why talk is important. *English Teaching: Practice and Critique* 9(2): 7–10. Available at <http://education.waikato.ac.nz/research/files/etpc/files/2010v9n2art1.pdf>. Accessed 13 February 2013.

Bauman, Zygmunt (1993). Ponowoczesne wzory osobowe. *Studia Socjologiczne* 2 (129): 7–31.

Bauman, Zygmunt (2011). Moda – wymienna tożsamość – utopia na dziś: O niektórych tendencjach kultury XXI stulecia. In: Zygmunt Bauman. *Kultura w płynnej nowoczesności*. Warszawa: Agora, SA, 35–49.

Beck, Ulrich (2003). *Risk Society: Towards a New Modernity*. Trans. Mark Ritter. London: Sage Publications.

Bentley, Lesley. *Paulo Freire*. Available at <http://www.ptoweb.org/freire.html>. Accessed 7 October 2012.

Bereś, Jerzy, Jacek Kasprzycki, Paweł Łubowski (2009). Interview: dokumenty rzeczowe. *Artluk* 4: 58–65.

Bernstein, Basil (2003). *Class, Codes and Control*. Vol. 1: *Theoretical Studies towards a Sociology of Language*. London: Routledge.

Blaszk, Martin (2009). Ethnodrama, action research and adaptation – some considerations in choosing a research method. *Problemy Wczesnej Edukacji* 10 (2): 82–91.

Blaszk, Martin (2017). *A Space for Happening in Education: An Empirical Study*. Frankfurt am Main: Peter Lang.

Boal, Augusto (1985). *Theatre of the Oppressed*. New York: Theatre Communications Group.

Boal, Augusto (1998). *Games for Actors and Non-actors*. Trans. Adrian Jackson. London: Routledge.

Bolt, Barbara (2004). *Art Beyond Representation: The Performative Power of the Image*. London: I.B. Tauris.

Borowski, Wiesław (1982). *Tadeusz Kantor*. Warszawa: Wydawnictwa Artystycznej Filmowe.

Bourdieu, Pierre (2011). The Forms of Capital. In: Imre Szeman, Timothy Kapsoy (eds.). *Cultural Theory: An Anthology*. Chichester: Wiley, Blackwell. 81–93.

Bruner, Jerome (1983). *Child's Talk: Learning to Use Language*. Oxford: Oxford University Press.

Bruner, Jerome (1999). *The Culture of Education*. Cambridge: Harvard University Press.

Buber, Martin (1937). *I and Thou*. Trans. Ronald Gregor Smith. Edinburgh: T. & T. Clark.

Burrell, Gibson, Gareth Morgan (1979). *Sociological Paradigms and Organisational Analysis*. London: Heinemann Educational Books.

Burzyński, Tadeusz, Zbigniew Osiński (1978). *Laboratorium Grotowskiego*. Warszawa: Interpress.

Certeau, Michel de (1988). *The Practice of Everyday Life*. Berkeley: University of California Press.

Clopper, Lawrence M. (2001). *Drama, Play, and Game: English Festive Culture in the Medieval and Early Modern Period*. Chicago: The University of Chicago Press.

Cohen, Louis, Lawrence Manion (1996). *Research Methods in Education.* London: Routledge.

Constantine, David, Helen Constantine (2011). *Poetry and the State.* Series 3, 15. Available at <http://www.mptmagazine.com/editorial/series-3-no15--poetry-and-the-state-145/>. Accessed 27 April 2012.

Czaja, Iwona, Monika Nęcka (2010). Sposoby rozumienia sztuki i obcowania z nią w świetle koncepcji inteligencji wielorakich. In: Ewa Smak, Stanisława Włoch (eds.). *Pedagogika kreatywna wyzwaniem edukacji XXI wieku.* Opole: Wydawnictwo Uniwersytetu Opolskiego, 191–200.

Dąbrowski, Kazimierz (1988). *Pasja rozwoju.* Warszawa: Studencka Oficyna Wydawnicza ZSP, Alma-Press.

Deleuze, Gilles (1993). *The Fold: Leibniz and the Baroque.* Trans. Tom Conley. London: The Athlone Press.

Deleuze, Gilles, Félix Guattari (1987). *A Thousand Plateaus: Capitalism and Schizophrenia.* Vol. 2. Trans. Brian Massumi. Minneapolis: University of Minnesota Press.

Delors, Jacques et al. (1996). *Learning: The Treasure Within. Report to UNESCO of the International Commission on Education for the Twenty-First Century. Highlights.* Paris: UNESCO Publishing.

Dembiński, Mariusz (2005). *Rytualne oblicze lekcji.* Kraków: Oficyna Wydawnicza Impuls.

Dewey, John (1956). *The Child and the Curriculum. The School and Society.* Chicago: The University of Chicago Press.

Dewey, John (1958). *Art as Experience.* New York: Capricorn Books.

Dewey, John (1966). *Democracy and Education.* New York: The Free Press, Macmillan Publishing Co., Inc.

Domańska, Ewa (2007). *"Zwrot performatywny" we współczesnej humanistyce.* Teksty Drugie 5: 48–61. Available at <http://www.staff.amu.edu.pl/~ewa/Domanska,%20Zwrot%20performatywny%20we%20wspolczesnej%20humanistyce.pdf>. Accessed 20 September 2009.

Dziamski, Grzegorz (1997). Happening performance. In: Grzegorz Dziamski (ed.). *Od awangardy do postmodernizmu.* Warszawa: Instytut Kultury, 349–368.

Dziamski, Grzegorz (2010). Radykalizacja demokracji: sztuka w sferze publicznej. In: Dorota Koczanowicz, Mateusz Skrezkowski (eds.). *Między estetyzacją a emancypacją. Praktyki artystyczne w przestrzeni publicznej.* Wrocław: Wydawnictwo Naukowe Dolnośląskiej Szkoły Wyższej, 15–26.

Epstein, Seymour (2003). Cognitive-experiential self-theory: An integrative theory of personality. In: Theodore Millon, Melvin J. Lerner (eds.). *Handbook of Psychology*, Vol. 5. New Jersey: John Wiley & Sons, Inc., 159–184.

Erikson, Erik H. (1963). *Childhood and Society*. New York: W.W. Norton and Company Inc.

European Union Key Competences for Schooling (2009) Available at <http://ec.europa.eu/education/school-education/doc830_en.htm>. Accessed 8 September 2009.

European Union Policy Document Key Competences for Schooling (2009). Available at<http://ec.europa.eu/education/lifelong-learning-policy/doc28_en.htm>. Accessed 8 September 2009.

Fatyga, Barbara (2001). Pseudo-kulturai pseudo-tożsamość, czyli czego nie przewidziała Margaret Mead. In: Barbara Fatyga, Anna Tyszkiewicz (eds.). *Normalność i normalka. Próba zastosowania pojęcia normalności do badań młodzieży*. Warszawa: Ośrodek Badań Młodzieży, 94–119.

Freire, Paulo (2000). *Pedagogy of the Oppressed*. New York: Continuum.

Galewska-Kustra, Marta (2009). Studium przypadku w pedagogicznych badaniach nad twórczością. W poszukiwaniu praktycznych zastosowań metody. In: Krzysztof J. Szmidt (ed.). *Metody pedagogicznych badań nad twórczością*. Łódź: Wydawnictwo Akademii Humanistyczno-Ekonomicznej w Łodzi, 225–275.

Gardner, Howard (1999). *Frames of Mind: The Theory of Multiple Intelligences*. USA: Basic Books.

Gardner, Howard et al. (2009). *The Theory of Multiple Intelligences*. Available at <https://howardgardner01.files.wordpress.com/2012/06/443-davis-christodoulou-seider-mi-article.pdf>. Accessed 7 August 2012.

Garoian, Charles R. (1999). *Performing Pedagogy: Toward an Art of Politics*. Albany: State University of New York Press.

Geertz, Clifford (1980). Blurred genres: The refiguration of social thought. *The American Scholar* 49(2): 165–179.

Gennap, Arnold van, (2004). *The Rites of Passage*. Trans. Monika B. Vizedom, Gabriella L. Caffee. London: Routledge.

Giroux, Henry A. (2011). *On Critical Pedagogy*. New York: Continuum International Publishing Group.

Goldberg, Roselee (1990). *Performance Art: From Futurism to the Present*. London: Thames and Hudson.

Gołębniak, Bogusława D. (2007). Szkoła wspomagająca rozwój. In: Zbigniew Kwieciński, Bogusław Śliwerski (eds.). *Pedagogika: Podręcznik akademicki*. Warszawa: Wydawnictwo Naukowe PWN, 98–122.

Greaves, Tom (2010). *Starting with Heidegger*. London: Continuum International Publishing Group.

Gross, Richard D., Paul Humphreys (1993). *Psychology. The Science of Mind and Behaviour.* London: Hodder & Stoughton.

Guba, Egon G., Yvonne S. Lincoln (2005). Paradigmatic controversies, contradictions, and emerging confluences. In: Norman K. Denzin, Yvonna S. Lincoln (eds.). *The Sage Handbook of Qualitative Research.* 3rd ed. Thousand Oaks, Sage Publications Ltd., 191–215.

Harrison, Charles, Paul Wood (eds.) (1994). *Art in Theory 1900–1990: An Anthology of Changing Ideas.* Oxford: Blackwell.

Heddon, Deirdre, Jane Milling (2006). *Devising Performance.* Hampshire: Palgrave Macmillan.

Herbert, Simon (1994). Bread and Circuses. In: Nicola Hodges (ed.). *Performance Art Into The 90s.* London: Art & Design, 6–35.

Heron, John, Peter Reason (1997). A participatory inquiry paradigm. *Qualitative Inquiry* 3(3): 274–294. Available at <http://www.cnr.uidaho.edu/CSS506/506%20Readings/Participatory%20inquiry%20paradigm_Heron%20%20Reason_1997.pdf>. Accessed 6 September 2010.

Hoffman, Marcelo (2011). Disciplinary power. In: Dianna Taylor (ed.). *Michel Foucault: Key Concepts.* Durham: Acumen Publishing Limited, 27–39.

Huizinga, Johan (1970). *Homo Ludens: A Study of the Play Element in Culture.* London: Paladin.

Hurło, Lucyna, Dorota Klus-Stańska, Majka Łojko (eds.) (2009). *Paradygmaty współczesnej dydaktyki.* Kraków: Oficyna Wydawnicza Impuls.

Jackson, Philip W. (1998). *John Dewey and the Lessons of Art.* New Haven: Yale University Press.

Kantor, Tadeusz (2005). *Metamorfozy: Teksty o latach 1934–1974.* Wrocław: Zakład Narodowym. Ossolińskich / Kraków: Ośrodek Dokumentacji Sztuki Tadeusza Kantora Cricoteka.

Kelly, Jeff (ed.) (2003). *Essays on the Blurring of Art and Life.* Berkley: University of California Press.

Kemp-Welch, Klara (2006). Excursions in Communist Reality: Tadeusz Kantor's Impossible Happenings. *Object. Graduate Research and Reviews in the History of Art and Culture* 8: 45–65.

Kenney, Padraic (2002). *A Carnival of Revolution: Central Europe 1989.* Princeton: Princeton University Press.

Kenney, Padraic (2011). What's so funny about post-communism? In: Barbara Górska, Benjamin Koschalka (eds.). *Happening against Communism by the Orange Alternative*. Kraków: International Cultural Centre, 100–113.

Kincheloe, Joe L. *Bricolage and the Quest for Multiple Perspectives: New Approaches to Research in Ethnic Studies*. Available at <http://209.85.229.132/search?q=cache:GpErcOixaeUJ:www.freireproject.org/articles/no e%252065/Research/Bricolage.doc+bricolage+in+quantitative+research&cd=10&hl=pl&ct=clnk&gl=pl>. Accessed 1 January 2010.

Kincheloe, Joe L., Peter McLaren (2005). Rethinking critical theory and qualitative research. In: Norman K. Denzin, Yvonna S. Lincoln (eds.). *The Sage Handbook of Qualitative Research*. 3rd ed. Thousand Oaks, Sage Publications Ltd., 303–342.

Kirby, Michael (1966). *Happenings: An Illustrated Anthology*. New York: E.P. Dutton & Co., Inc.

Klus-Stańska, Dorota (2002). *Konstruowanie wiedzy w szkole*. Olsztyn: Wydawnictwo Uniwersytetu Warmińsko-Mazurskiego.

Klus-Stańska, Dorota (2006). Obszary zgodna twórczość dziecięcą we wczesnej edukacji. In: Ewa Szatan, Dorota Bronk (eds.). *Gdyby Einstein współcześnie chodził do szkoły. Dziecko i twórczość w pedagogice wczesnoszkolnej*. Gdańsk: Wydawnictwo Uniwersytetu Gdańskiego, 57–68.

Klus-Stańska, Dorota (2009). Dyskursy pedagogiki wczesnoszkolnej. In: Dorota Klus-Stańska, Maria Szczepska-Pustkowska (eds.). *Pedagogika wczesnoszkolna – dyskursy, problemy, rozwiązania*. Warszawa: Wydawnictwa Akademickie Profesjonalne, 25–78.

Klus-Stańska, Dorota (2012). Wiedza, która zniewala – transmisyjne tradycje w szkolnej edukacji. *Forum Oświatowe* 1 (46): 21–40.

Kolankiewicz, Leszek (1978). *Na drodze do kultury czynnej: O działalności instytutu Grotowskiego: Teatr Laboratorium w latach 1970–1977*. Wrocław: Instytut Aktora –Teatr Laboratorium.

Krasoń, Katarzyna (2013). *Cielesność aktu tworzenia w teatrze ruchu*. Kraków: TAIWPN Universitas.

Krauze-Sikorska, Hanna (2006). *Edukacja przez sztukę o edukacyjnych wartościach artystycznej twórczości dziecka*. Poznań: Wydawnictwo Uniwersytet im. Adama Mickiewicza w Poznaniu.

Królica, Maria (2006). *Drama i happening w edukacji przedszkolnej*. Kraków: Oficyna Wydawnicza Impuls.

Kruk, Jolanta (2008). *Doświadczenie, reprezentacja i działanie wśród rzeczy i przedmiotów. Projektowanie edukacyjne*. Gdańsk: Wydawnictwo Uniwersytetu Gdańskiego.

Kupisiewicz, Czesław (2010). Szkoła alternatywna - definicje, rodzaje, ocena, perspektywy rozwoju. In: Bogusław Śliwerski (ed.). *Pedagogika alternatywna w XXI wieku.* Kraków: Oficyna Wydawnicza Impuls, 17–25.

Kwaśnica, Robert (1995). Ku dialogi w pedagogice. *Acta Universitatis Wratislaviensis* 1747/*Prace Pedagogiczne* CVIII: 11–27.

Kwiatkowska, Henryka (2006). Nauczyciel - myślenie kategoriami sprawstwa wychowawczego. In: Małgorzata Bogaj (ed.). *Współczesne gimnazjum w Polsce: nadzieje i zagrożenia.* Kielce: Wydawnictwo Uczelniane, Wszechnica Świętokrzyska; Warszawa, IBE, 57–63.

Lamont, Michelle, Annette Lareau (1988). Cultural capital: Allusions, gaps and glissandos in recent theoretical developments. *Sociological Theory* 6 (2): 153–168.

Levinas, Emmanuel (1996). Martin Heidegger and ontology. *Diacritics.* 26/1: 11–32.

Limon, Jerzy (2006). *Piąty wymiar teatru.* Gdańsk: słowo/obraz terytoria.

Marciniak, Zbigniew. O potrzebie reform programowej kształcenia ogólnego. In: *Podstawa programowa, tom 7 - Edukacja artystyczna w szkole podstawowej, gimnazjumi liceum.* MEN. Available at <http://195.136.199.90/images/stories/pdf/Reforma/7a.pdf>. Accessed 10 March 2013.

Matynia, Elżbieta (2009). *Performative Democracy.* Boulder: Paradigm Publishers.

McLaren, Peter (1993). *Schooling as a Ritual Performance: Towards a Political Economy of Educational Symbols and Gestures.* New York: Routledge.

Mead, Margaret (1970). *Culture and Commitment: A Study of the Generation Gap.* New York: Natural History Press/Doubleday.

Melosik, Zbyszko (2007). Pedagogika pragmatyzmu. In: Zbigniew Kwieciński, Bogusław Śliwerski (eds.). *Pedagogika: Podręcznik akademicki* 1. Warszawa: Wydawnictwo Naukowe PWN, 307–323.

Melosik, Zbyszko, Tomasz Szkudlarek (2009). *Kultura, tożsamości, edukacja: Migotanie znaczeń.* Kraków: Impuls.

Mendel, Maria (2006). Pedagogika miejsca i animacja na miejsce wrażliwa. In: Maria Mendel (ed.). *Pedagogika miejsca.* Wrocław: Dolnośląska Szkoła Wyższa Edukacji TWP, 21–37.

Mendel, Maria (2007). *Społeczeństwo i rytuał: Heterotopia bezdomności.* Toruń: Wydawnictwo Adam Marszałek.

Miciukiewicz, Konrad (2006). Miasto jako społeczna reprodukcja przestrzeni i kontrprzestrzeni miejsc. In: Maria Mendel (ed.). *Pedagogika miejsca.* Wrocław: Dolnośląska Szkoła Wyższa Edukacji TWP, 209–238.

Mienczakowski, Jim (2008). Ethnodrama: Performed research – limitations and potential. In: Paul Atkinson et al. (eds.). *The Handbook of Ethnography*. Los Angeles: Sage, 468–476.

Morawski, Stefan (1971a). Happening (1): Rodowód – charakter – funkcje. *Dialog 9*: 109–144.

Morawski, Stefan (1971b). Happening (2). Rodowód – charakter – funkcje. *Dialog 10*: 117–144.

Morgan, Robert C. (2012). The early happenings: When performance met art in New York. *White Hot Magazine*. Available at <http://whitehotmagazine.com/articles/met-art-in-new-york/2487>. Accessed 4 April 2012.

Mytkowska, Joanna (2000). The object that is got back by chance. In: Jarosław Suchan (ed.). *Tadeusz Kantor: Niemożliwe. Impossible*. Kraków: Bunkier Sztuki, 55–66.

Narayan, Swati (2012). *Education for All: Beyond 2015. Mapping Current International Actions to Define the Post-2015 Education and Development Agendas*. Paris: UNESCO.

Nęcka, Edward (1994). *TRoP... Twórcze rozwiązywanie problemów*. Kraków: Oficyna Wydawnicza Impuls.

Nęcka, Edward (1999). *Proces twórczy i jego ograniczenia*. Kraków: Oficyna Wydawnicza Impuls.

Nowicka, Marzena (2009). Oblicza szkolnej socjalizacji. In: Dorota Klus-Stańska, Maria Szczepska-Pustkowska (eds.). *Pedagogika wczesnoszkolna – dyskursy, problemy, rozwiązania*. Warszawa: Wydawnictwa Akademickiej Profesjonalne, 261–290.

Nowicka, Marzena (2010). *Socjalizacja na lekcjach w klasach początkowych. Praktyki – Przestrzenie – Konceptualizacje*. Toruń: Wydawnictwo Adam Marszałek.

O'Brien, Rory (2001). Um exame da abordagem metodológica da pesquisaação [An Overview of the Methodological Approach of Action Research]. In: Roberto Richardson (ed.). *Teoria e Prática da Pesquisa Ação*. João Pessoa, Brazil: Universidade Federal da Paraíba. Available at <http://www.web.ca/~robrien/papers/arfinal.html>. Accessed 25 November 2009.

Osiński, Zbigniew (2009). *Źródła, inspiracje, konteksty*. Gdańsk: Słowo/obraz terytoria.

Osterman, Karen F. (1990). Reflective practice: A new agenda for education. *Education and Urban Society*. 22/2: 133–152.

Pankowska, Krystyna (2000). *Pedagogika dramy: Teoria i praktyka*. Warszawa: Wydawnictwo Akademickie Żak.

Paterson, Doug. *Augusto Boal*. Available at <http://www.ptoweb.org/freire.html>. Accessed 7 October 2012.

Patraka, Vivien M. (1999). *Spectacular Suffering: Theatre, Fascism, and the Holocaust*. Bloomington: Indiana University Press.

Pawluczuk, Włodzimierz (1978a). *Naprawianie świata*. Warszawa: Ludowa Spółdzielnia Wydawnicza.

Pawluczuk, Włodzimierz (1978b). *Żywioł i forma: Wstęp do badań empirycznych nad kulturą współczesną*. Warszawa: Państwowy Instytut Wydawniczy.

Pawłowski, Tadeusz (1982). *Happening*. Warszawa: Wiedza Powszechna.

Pilch, Tadeusz, Teresa Bauman (2001). *Zasady badań pedagogicznych: Strategie ilościowych i jakościowe*. Warszawa: Wydawnictwo Akademickie Żak.

Pleśniarowicz, Krzysztof (1997). *Kantor*. Wrocław: Wydawnictwo Dolnośląskie.

Potulicka, Eugenia, Joanna Rutkowiak (eds.) (2012). *Neoliberalne uwikłania edukacji*. Kraków: Oficyna Wydawnicza Impuls.

Quirk, Randolph (ed.) (1991). *Longman Dictionary of the English Language*. New Edition. Harlow: Longman.

Reason, Peter (1994). Three approaches to participative inquiry. In: Norman K. Denzin, Yvonne S. Lincoln (eds.). *Handbook of Qualitative Research*. London: Sage Publications, Inc., 324–339.

Rubacha, Krzysztof (2007a). Budowanie teorii pedagogicznych. In: Zbigniew Kwieciński, Bogusław Śliwerski (eds.). *Pedagogika: Podręcznik Akademicki* 1. Warszawa: Wydawnictwo Naukowe PWN, 59–68.

Rubacha, Krzysztof (2007b). Nowe kategorie pojęciowe współczesnej teorii wychowania. In: Zbigniew Kwieciński, Bogusław Śliwerski (eds.). *Pedagogika: Podręcznik akademicki* 2. Warszawa: Wydawnictwo Naukowe PWN, 59–67.

Rutkowiak, Joanna (ed.) (1997). *Uczenie się od outsidera: Perspektywa europejskiej współpracy edukacyjnej*. Kraków: Oficyna Wydawnicza Impuls.

Rutkowiak, Joanna (2012). Czy istnieje edukacyjny program ekonomii korporacyjnej? In: Eugenia Potulicka, Joanna Rutkowiak (eds.). *Neoliberalne uwikłania edukacji*. Kraków: Oficyna Wydawnicza Impuls, 13–37.

Sadoń-Osowiecka, Teresa (2009a). Bricolage jako konstruktywistyczne podejście do badań edukacyjnych. *Problemy Wczesnej Edukacji* 2 (10): 72–81.

Sadoń-Osowiecka, Teresa (2009b). *Konstruowanie wiedzy geograficznej w klasach gimnazjalnych: Możliwości i zaniedbania*. Kraków: Oficyna Wydawnicza Impuls.

Sajdak, Anna (2008). *Edukacja kreatywna*. Kraków: Wydawnictwo WAM.

Schechner, Richard (1982). *The End of Humanism: Writings on Performance*. New York: Performing Arts Journal Publications.

Schechner, Richard (1988). *Performance Theory.* New York: Routledge.

Schneider, Rebecca (1997). *The Explicit Body in Performance.* London: Routledge.

Shmueli, Sandra (2003). 'Flash mob' craze spreads. CNN. Available at <http://edition.cnn.com/2003/TECH/internet/08/04/flash.mob/>. Accessed 15 August 2014.

Shrum, Wesley, Ricardo Duque, Timothy Brown (2005). Digital video as research practice: methodology for the millennium. *Journal of Research Practice.* 1/1, Article M4. Available at <http://quimera.tv/wp-content/uploads/2007/03/digital-video-as-research-practice.pdf>. Accessed 9 December 2009.

Słownik-online (2005). Available at <http://www.słownik-online.pl/kopalinski/631F766D39B3CCE8C12565DC004D64F0.php>. Accessed 18 November 2005.

Spencer, Jenny S. (2001). Performance art as progressive education – performing pedagogy: Toward an art of politics – Review. *Art Journal.* 60/1: 102–104.

Suchan, Jarosław (2000). Happening as a Ready-made. In: Jarosław Suchan (ed.). *Tadeusz Kantor. Niemożliwe. Impossible.* Kraków: Bunkier Sztuki, 87–104.

Swartz, David (1997). *Culture and Power: The Sociology of Pierre Bourdieu.* Chicago: The University of Chicago Press.

Szatan, Ewa (2007). Przygotowanie nauczycieli do edukacji muzycznej dziecka w kontekście standardów kształcenia studentów. In: Ewa Szatan (ed.). *Wybrane problem wczesnej edukacji artystycznej.* Gdańsk: Fundacja Rozwoju Uniwersytetu Gdańskiego, 7–15.

Szatan, Ewa, Dorota Bronk (2006). Wstęp. In: Ewa Szatan, Dorota Bronk (eds.). *Gdyby Einstein Współcześnie chodził do szkoły. Dziecko i twórczość w pedagogice wczesnoszkolnej.* Gdańsk: Wydawnictwo Uniwersytetu Gdańskiego, 7–10.

Szkudlarek, Tomasz (2009). *Wiedza i wolność w pedagogice amerykańskiego postmodernizmu.* Kraków: Oficyna Wydawnictwo Impuls.

Szkudlarek, Tomasz, Bogusław Śliwerski (1991). *Wyzwania pedagogiki krytycznej i antypedagogiki.* Kraków: Niezależne Wydawnictwo Harcerskie Impuls.

Szmidt, Krzysztof J. (2007). *Pedagogika twórczości.* Gdańsk: Gdańskie Wydawnictwo Psychologiczne.

Szuścik, Urszula (2007). Rozważania o plastyce i muzyce w kształceniu ucznia. In: Ewa Szatan (ed.). *Wybrane problemy wczesnej edukacji artystycznej.* Gdańsk: Fundacja Rozwoju Uniwersytetu Gdańskiego, 55–62.

Szymański, Mirosław S. (2010). *O metodzie projektów.* Warszawa: Wydawnictwo Akademickie ŻAK.

Śliwerski, Bogusław (2009). *Problemy współczesnej edukacji. Dekonstrukcja polityki oświatowej IIIRP.* Warszawa: Wydawnictwa Akademickie i Profesjonalne.

Śliwerski, Bogusław (ed.) (2010). *Pedagogika alternatywna w XXI wieku.* Kraków: Oficyna Wydawnicza Impuls.

Taylor, Dianne (2011). Practices of the self. In: Dianne Taylor (ed.). *Michael Foucault: Key Concepts.* Durham: Acumen Publishing Ltd., 173–186.

Trzebiński, Jerzy (2002). *Narracja jako sposób rozumienia świata.* Gdańsk: Gdańskie Wydawnictwo Psychologiczne.

Turner, Victor (1991). *The Ritual Process: Structure and Anti-Structure.* New York: Cornell University Press.

Tyszka, Juliusz (ed.) (2003). *Świat na opak 10 lat Teatru Strefa Ciszy / The World Turned Upside Down or 10 Years of Teatr Strefa Ciszy.* Poznań: Wydawnictwo Kontekst.

Wasik, Bill (2006). My Crowd. Or, Phase 5: A report from the inventor of the flash mob. *Harper's Magazine.* Available at <http://harpers.org/archive/2006/03/my-crowd/>. Accessed 15 August 2014.

Wawrzyniak-Śliwska, Magdalena (2007). Educational schizophrenia - what we claim to believe and what we practice in the classroom. *Problemy Wczesnej Edukacji* 1/2 (5/6): 172–179.

Witkowski, Lech (1997). *Edukacja wobec sporów o (po)nowoczesność.* Warszawa: Instytut Badań Edukacyjnych.

Witkowski, Lech (2000). *Uniwersalizm pogranicza.* Toruń: Wydawnictwo Adam Marszałek.

Witkowski, Lech (2007). Typy dialogu w kulturze a strategie edukacyjne. In: Lech Witkowski (ed.). *Edukacja i humanistyka: Nowe (kon)teksty dla nowoczesnych nauczyciel II. Tryptyku edukacyjnego.* Warszawa: Instytut Badań Edukacyjnych, 51–62.

Wittgenstein, Ludwig (2009). *Philosophical Investigations.* 4th ed. Trans. Gertrude E.M. Anscombe, Peter M.S. Hacker, Joachim Schutte. Chichester: Blackwell Publishing Ltd.

Wood, David (1998). *How Children Think and Learn.* Oxford: Blackwell.

Zawadzki, Michał (2009). Dlaczego powieść może stać się narzędziem budowania tożsamości? Rozważania nad ponowoczesną kondycją ludzką przy wykorzystaniu narracji powieściowej Hermanna Hessego. *Humanicus: Academic Journal of Humanities, Social Sciences and Philosophy* 2: 5–37. Available at <http://www.humanicus.org/global/issues/humanicus-2-2009.pdf>. Accessed 8 September 2009.

Ziołowicz, Katarzyna (2006). Problemy edukacji plastycznej w gimnazjum. In: Małgorzata Bogaj (ed.). *Współczesne gimnazjum w Polsce: Nadzieje i zagrożenia.* Kielce: Wydawnictwo Uczelniane, Wszechnica Świętokrzyska; Warszawa: IBE, 317–332.

Author index

Subject Index

www.ingramcontent.com/pod-product-compliance
Ingram Content Group UK Ltd.
Pitfield, Milton Keynes, MK11 3LW, UK
UKHW041827031026
15587UKWH00002B/607

9 783631 722428